The Celestial Dancers

The Celestial Dancers: Manipuri Dance on Australian Stage charts the momentous journey of the popularization of Manipur's Hindu dances in Australia.

Tradition has it that the people of Manipur, a northeastern state of India, are descended from the celestial *gandharvas,* dance and music blessed among them as a God's gift. The intricately symbolic Hindu dances of Manipur in their original religious forms were virtually unseen and unknown outside India until an Australian impresario, Louise Lightfoot, brought them to the stage in the 1950s. Her experimental changes through a pioneering collaboration with dancers Rajkumar Priyagopal Singh and Ibetombi Devi modernized Manipuri dance for presentation on a global stage. This partnership moved Manipur's Hindu dances from the sphere of ritualistic temple practice to a formalized stage art abroad. Amit Sarwal chronicles how this movement, as in the case of other prominent Indian classical dances and dancers, enabled both Manipuri dance and dancers to gain recognition worldwide.

This book is ideal for anyone with an interest in Hindu temple dance, Manipur dance, cross-cultural collaborations and the globalizing of Indian Classical Dance. *The Celestial Dancers* is a comprehensive study of how an exceptional Hindu dance form developed on the global stage.

Amit Sarwal is the Founding Convenor of Australia-India Interdisciplinary Research Network and an Affiliate Member of the Contemporary Histories Research Group at Deakin University. He has served as the Deputy Head of School (Research, Innovation and Postgraduate Affairs) in the School of Pacific Arts, Communication and Education at the University of the South Pacific in Fiji. He is the author of *Labels and Locations* (2015), *South Asian Diaspora Narratives* (2016/2017) and *The Dancing God* (2020).

Routledge Advances in Theatre and Performance Studies

This series is our home for cutting-edge, upper-level scholarly studies and edited collections. Considering theatre and performance alongside topics such as religion, politics, gender, race, ecology and the avant-garde, titles are characterized by dynamic interventions into established subjects and innovative studies on emerging topics.

Marginality Beyond Return
US Cuban Performances in the 1980s and 1990s
Lillian Manzor

Staging Rebellion in the Musical, Hair
Marginalised Voices in Musical Theatre
Sarah Browne

Shakespeare and Tourism
Valerie Pye, Robert Ormsby

Contemporary Chinese Queer Performance
Hongwei Bao

Rapa Nui Theatre
Staging Indigenous Identities in Easter Island
Moira S. Fortin Cornejo

For more information about this series, please visit: https://www.routledge.com/Routledge-Advances-in-Theatre--Performance-Studies/book-series/RATPS

The Celestial Dancers

Manipuri Dance on Australian Stage

Amit Sarwal

Routledge
Taylor & Francis Group

LONDON AND NEW YORK

First published 2022
by Routledge
4 Park Square, Milton Park, Abingdon, Oxon OX14 4RN

and by Routledge
605 Third Avenue, New York, NY 10158

Routledge is an imprint of the Taylor & Francis Group, an informa business

© 2022 Amit Sarwal

The right of Amit Sarwal to be identified as the author of this work
has been asserted in accordance with sections 77 and 78 of the
Copyright, Designs and Patents Act 1988.

All rights reserved. No part of this book may be reprinted or
reproduced or utilized in any form or by any electronic, mechanical
or other means, now known or hereafter invented, including
photocopying and recording, or in any information storage or
retrieval system, without permission in writing from the publishers.

Trademark notice: Product or corporate names may be trademarks or
registered trademarks, and are used only for identification and
explanation without intent to infringe.

British Library Cataloguing-in-Publication Data
A catalogue record for this book is available from the British Library

Library of Congress Cataloging-in-Publication Data
Names: Sarwal, Amit, author.
Title: The celestial dancers : Manipuri dance on Australian stage /
Amit Sarwal.
Description: Abingdon, Oxon ; New York, NY : Routledge, 2023. |
Series: Routledge advances in theatre and performance studies |
Includes bibliographical references and index.
Identifiers: LCCN 2022005522 (print) | LCCN 2022005523
(ebook) | ISBN 9781032069449 (hardback) | ISBN
9781032070650 (paperback) | ISBN 9781003205203 (ebook)
Subjects: LCSH: Dance--India--Manipur. | Dance--Religious
aspects--Hinduism. | Lightfoot, Louise. | Singh, Rajkumar Priyagopal.
| Devi, Ibetombi. | Choreography--Australia--History--20th century.
Classification: LCC GV1694.M3 S27 2023 (print) | LCC
GV1694.M3 (ebook) | DDC 792.80954/17--dc23/eng/20220321
LC record available at https://lccn.loc.gov/2022005522
LC ebook record available at https://lccn.loc.gov/2022005523

ISBN: 978-1-032-06944-9 (hbk)
ISBN: 978-1-032-07065-0 (pbk)
ISBN: 978-1-003-20520-3 (ebk)

DOI: 10.4324/9781003205203

Typeset in Bembo
by MPS Limited, Dehradun

For Reema, Mishank and Saavi

Contents

Figures

Glossary

Abhinaya   gesture language: emotions and stories conveyed via hand-gestures and facial expressions
Adbhuta   marvellous
Advaita Vedanta   a school in Hinduism
Aharya   dress
Ahimsa   non-violence
Angika   body gestures
Anugraha   salvation
Anuraag   grace of god
Apsaras   celestial nymphs
Aranyakas   the philosophy behind ritual sacrifice in the Vedas
Asamyukta hastas   single hand gestures
Avirbhava   creation
Bazaar   market
Bhagtans   female dancers from the bhagtan community in Rajasthan
Bhakti   theistic devotion
Bhartiya Shastriya Nritya   Indian Classical Dance
Bhava   mood or feeling (accompanying rasa)
Bhayanaka   terrible
Bhramaris   kinds of pirouettes
Bols (or bol cholum)   dance syllables also used as percussion syllables
Brahmanas   commentaries on the Veda
Chautal (or chartal)   four claps that are strongly linked to the pakhawaj (barrel-shaped drums) tradition
Dakhina (or dakshina)   offering or tips
Dalits   Untouchables or members of the lower castes
Devadasi   a female servant of God who is dedicated to the temple deity
Dvapara   after two
Gandharvas   heavenly beings in Hinduism and Buddhism
Gopi   milkmaid

Guru   teacher
Hasya   comic
Hindutva   Hinduness
Isthiti   preservation
Kalavangtis   women temple dancers
Kaliyug   the age of darkness
Karuna   pathos
Kathakali   classical dance style from Kerala
Khamba-thoibi (or Jagoi)   a dance performed as part of Lai Haraoba
Khari boli   a more Sanskritised form of Hindi
Kriyas   work of God
Kukis   the hill tribes of India and Myanmar related to Tibeto-Burman tribal people
Lai haraoba   a traditional festival dance celebrating deities and ancestors
Lasya   a dance performed by Goddess Parvathi expressing happiness and beauty
Laya   tempo in Indian classical music
Mahabharata   one of the major Sanskrit epic narrative of India
Maibi   a pre-Hindu ritualistic priestess dance
Manasika   the action of the mind
Mandalas   universe or modes of standing
Mani   a jewel
Manipuri   classical Indian dance style from the state of Manipur
Matthas   a Hindu monastery
Meitei goura Chaytonya   People of Manipur who follow Meitei and Hindu gods
Meitei marup   People of Manipur who follow traditional Meitei culture and God
Meiteis   Manipur's main ethnic group
Miah Meitei   the Meitei Muslims or people of Manipur who follow Islam
Mohiniattam   a female classical Indian dance style from Kerala
Moksha   salvation
Mridangam   a drum played on the sides, used in South Indian Carnatic classical music
Mudras   hand-gestures used both in abstract movement without any literal meaning, and for symbolic meaning, in telling stories and conveying emotions
Nagar badhus (or Nagar Vadhu)   a courtesan
Nagas   an ethnic group associated with northeastern parts of India especially Nagaland, Manipur, Arunachal Pradesh and Assam

Nataraj   the God of dance with iconic one leg raised up and pointing diagonally

Nautch   a dance performed by professional dancing girls

Navarasas   nine primary emotions (love, fear, laughter, valour, disgust, sorrow, anger, wonder, peace)

Nayaka   a hero

Nirhetuka   unconditional

Nritta hastas   ornate gestures

Nritta   rhythmic footwork in traditional Indian dance

Odissi   classical Indian dance style from the state of Orissa (Eastern India)

Parampurussharaartha   ultimate goal

Paratattva   ultimate reality

Parvas   an episode

Prakriti   nature

Pung Cholom (or Poong Cholom)   a drum dance usually performed as a prelude to the *Ras Lila*

Puranas   Hindu religious texts that contain narratives about the history of the Universe from creation to destruction

Purusha   omnipresent spirit

Rabindra Nritiya Natya   the group of three dance-dramas composed by poet laureate Rabindranath Tagore

Rabindra Sangit (or Rabindra Sangeet)   songs composed by poet laureate Rabindranath Tagore

Ras Lila (or Ras Leela)   a Vaishnavite dance drama about Radha and Krishna's love rasa: emotion or taste

Raudra   furious

Sabha   auditorium

Sahibs   elite Western visitors

Samhara   destruction

Samyukta hastas   combined hand gestures

Sanamahism   the traditional Meitei religion

Santa   tranquil

Saririka   bodily action

Sattvika   physical

Satya   the golden age

Shaiva   followers of Shiva

Shakta   followers of Devi

Shakti   female strength or Goddess

Sherwani   traditional Indian long coat

Slokas   Sanskrit verse stanzas

Smarta   followers of Brahman and all major deities

Sringara   love expressed in various manifestations – romantic, erotic, motherly, divine

Sthankas   modes of resting

Sutras   a rule or grammar of Hindu law and philosophy

Svabhavika   natural

Tabla   a set of two drums used in North Indian Hindustani classical music

Taṇḍava   a divine dance performed by Lord Shiva

Thang-ta   an ancient martial art form

Tirobhava   illusion

Treta   the third age

Upanishads   a collection of texts, religious, philosophical and historical

Utplavanas   kinds of leaps

Vadya visharad   Master Drummer or Master of Rhythm

Vaishnava (or *Vaishnavite*)   followers of Lord Vishnu

Varanshrama Dharma   duties performed according to the Hindu system of social division and stages in life

Veda   texts of knowledge (the four Vedas are: Rg Veda, the Samaveda, Yajurveda and the Atharvaveda)

Vibhatsa   disgust

Vira   heroic

Acknowledgements

I wish to express my sincere thanks to everyone who has, directly or indirectly, made possible the writing of this book.

First of all, I would like to acknowledge the support of the Music Archives of Monash University. A very special thanks to Prof. Margaret Kartomi, Prof. Cat Hope, Dr Anthea Skinner and Bronia Kornhauser for providing me their valuable time, support and help in acquiring the material and permission to reprint a large number of images from the Louise Lightfoot Collection.

The copyright to Louise Lightfoot's writings and images is held by Mary Louise Lightfoot. Heartfelt thanks to Mary for granting her kind permission to reprint images in this book. I am also very grateful for her valuable suggestions and feedback during the writing process. The project and related publications could not have been completed without the support of Mary.

All reasonable efforts have been made to find the copyright owners of the works reproduced in this book. If you have any information about copyright, please contact Dr Amit Sarwal (sarwal.amit@gmail.com) or the Music Archives of Monash University.

My gratitude to Tara Rajkumar, OAM, for her support to my work and or her permission to reprint image from her fabulous dance performance *Temple Dreaming*.

Special thanks are also due to Byron Aihara, of Seven Sisters Music (USA), for his kind permission to select and reprint images related to the Manipuri dance from his personal archives.

Thanks to the teams at the Library of Congress Prints and Photographs Division Washington, D.C., Los Angeles County Museum of Art, University of Hawai'i, Press Information Bureau (Government of India), Kalakeshtra Foundation, Indira Gandhi National Centre for the Arts, National Centre for the Performing Arts, Swatantryaveer Savarkar Rashtriya Smarak, National Library of Australia, National Archives of

Australia and the National Gallery of Victoria for granting their kind permission to reprint some of the images from their archives.

Many thanks to the editors and reviewers of journals *South Asian Popular Culture, Dance Chronicle* and *Dance Research* for their kind feedback on my articles. I am also grateful to Taylor and Francis and Cambridge Scholars Publishing for their permission to reprint material from my papers and books that they published originally.

Sincerest thanks are also due to Prof. Pal Ahluwalia, Prof. Ashish Mohan Khokar, Prof. Emerita Margaret Allen, Prof. Emeritus David Walker, Prof. David Lowe, Prof. Fethi Mansouri, Prof. Sudesh Mishra, Dr Sunil Kothari and my colleagues at Deakin University and the University of the South Pacific for their support.

I am grateful to Prof. Dhananjay Singh, of Jawaharlal Nehru University (New Delhi), for agreeing to read and give his valuable feedback on the chapter on Hinduism.

I appreciate the timely copy-editing and insightful comments provided by Dr Urvashi Vashist on my manuscript.

A special thanks to my friends Jitarth Jai Bharadwaj, Dr Mohit R. Pandit, Anjali Maindiratta, Harsha Sree, Vibhor Pandit, Shamsher Kainth, Ashrut Khatter, Hemesh Kumar, Karthik Arasu, Delys Paul, Anubha Sarkar and Gangotri Roy for helping me at various stages of the exhibition of my work.

To the publishing team, especially the anonymous reviewers, Laura Hussey and Swati Hindwan, a very big thank you for working on this book with professional skill and finesse.

Thanks to my extended family in India, USA, Canada and Germany for believing in my work and their unconditional love. I would like to express my most profound love, appreciation and thanks to my wife—Reema Sarwal; our children—Mishank Kansal Sarwal and Saavi Kansal Sarwal.

Introduction

Many books and research papers have been written on the history of Indian classical dance, the reception of Indian classical dance outside India, and Indian dance personalities on the global stage and in the Indian diaspora.[1] These have contributed immensely to the discipline of dance history and of the globalization of Indian classical dance. However, they have focused mostly on a single dance form—Bharatanatyam. In 2020, I published *The Dancing God: Staging Hindu Dance in Australia* that charted the sensational and historic journey of de-provincializing and popularizing Kerala's Kathakali dance form. I argued that in the late nineteenth and early twentieth centuries, colonialism, orientalism and nationalism came together in various combinations to transform the traditional Hindu temple dance into a global art form. The dynamic, nuanced and intensely alive form of Kathakali was introduced to Australian audiences and dancers by Louise Lightfoot in 1947. She and Ananda Shivaram together transformed the form from a mode of Hindu ritual performance to one of modern stage art: pliable and open to experimentation and interpretation (Figure 0.1). I concluded that this movement from India to Australia enabled both the authentic Hindu dance and its dancers to gain recognition worldwide and infused her persona with aspects of cultural guru and ambassador on the global stage.

The story of Manipuri dance coming to prominence on the global stage has not yet been told in its entirety either. This too is a dance form deeply rooted in the sacred texts of Hinduism and its temple dancing traditions. It was my keen interest in Australia-India cross-cultural connections, rather than an attachment with the dance practice or form, that inspired me to begin a two-year postdoctoral research project in January 2013, titled "Cross-Cultural Diplomacy: Indian Visitors to Australia, 1947 to 1980," at Deakin University, Australia. While writing about the role of public diplomacy and cross-cultural perceptions in Australia-India relations, scholars have highlighted a shared history that

DOI: 10.4324/9781003205203-1

Figure 0.1 Poster for Ananda Shivaram's dance recital at Repertory Theatre, Perth, Western Australia, 1948.

Source: Poster from the Louise Lightfoot Bequest, Monash University.

Photograph Courtesy: Music Archives of Monash University and Mary Louise Lightfoot.

underpins this relationship in all spheres.[2] Australian scholars have mostly focused on Australians gazing upon India.[3] However, the other side of the coin, the building of early Indian perceptions of Australia, has largely been neglected in this discourse.[4]

My project thus aimed at systematically examining how Australia and India viewed each other in the aftermath of decolonization. It was, particularly, a contextualization of key Indian visitors like noted dancers, journalists, writers and researchers from 1947 to 1980. Through research, I came to know of an Australian architect turned ballet teacher, Louise Lightfoot, who was known for her Indian-Australian dance and cultural collaborations. In the late 1970s, before her death, Louise donated her life's work—handwritten notes, photographs, negatives, scrapbooks, sketches, press cuttings, programmes, posters, brochures, letters, invoices, books, musical notes, maps, costumes, props and audio/video reels—in boxes and trunks to the Music Archives of Monash University. These trunks are evidence of Louise's dedication and passion towards making the best dance and artists of the world accessible to the Australian audience. In connection with this project, I accessed the Music Archives with the original intent of writing research papers on Indian dancers—Ananda Shivaram, Rajkumar Priyagopal Singh, Lakshman Singh and Ibetombi Devi—whose tours to Australia were organized by Louise from 1947 to 1976. By the end of 2013, as I delved deeper into this archival collection, I realized that despite her decades of hard work, dedication to Hindu dance and to creating awareness about India in Australia, Louise's collaboration with these Indian artists was relatively unknown in both the countries. To highlight Louise's work I edited and compiled her writing in a book *Louise Lightfoot in Search of India: An Australian Dancer's Experience* (2017). This book brought together thirty-three essays, reflecting her broader world-view as a dancer, choreographer and impresario. Louise's essays spoke to her various encounters with India and its diverse cultural conditions, beliefs and philosophies.

Much of the abovementioned work focused on two critical issues. The first is the de-provincializing of Hindu or Indian classical dance. The second is recovering Hindu or Indian classical dancers who saw themselves as cultural diplomats representing the religious traditions of ancient India on a secular global stage. For many Australians, India has always been a land of mysticism, magic, *moksha* (spiritual emancipation), a land of "sahibs, sadhus and spinners" or land of "Jadoowallahs, Jugglers and Jinns," as the titles of 2009 and 2018 Australian books on India suggest.[5] Indian spirituality and philosophy, reflected through the books such as *Bhagavad Gita,* has also captured the imagination of Australian intellectuals and writers. Further, there are many shared commonalities between the two countries: a history of British imperialism, the English language, trade and a love of cricket. What is less commonly known is that India was a lifeline for colonial Australia.[6] As part of the British colonists' world, Australia made its first trade links with India. Recent sociological, anthropological and genetic studies have thrown light on linguistic and other similarities between Aborigines and Andamanese tribes. They also point to earlier links, between pre-colonial Australia and the Indian subcontinent, such as trade between Aborigines and Makassar seamen. Later, with the beginning of British colonialism the Ghans and hawkers, who connected the Australian outback with its towns and cities, were "brought" from Northern India.[7] Eminent lawyer John Lang, who represented the Indian Queen of Jhansi Lakshmibai in court against the British, was the first Australian-born novelist.[8] The rum of the Rum Rebellion or the Great Rebellion of 1808 came from India.[9] The popular and common habit of drinking tea, closely associated with British life in the tropics, came from India—an Australian named James "Rajah" Inglis, made a fortune through his "Billy Tea" brand.[10] Similarly, in India, Walers—the great horses of the British Raj used in

Polo—were imported from New South Wales, and the Mahalaxmi Racecourse in Mumbai was designed after Caulfield and Randwick Racecourses. The last Nizam of Hyderabad made Western Australia his home for some time.[11] Owing to such connections, even today, some Australian towns and pastoral properties carry Indian names reflecting a deep if sometimes fractured connection between colonial India and white Australia.[12]

The Australian settler colonies—the white man's club—and India had a very different relationship to the British Empire.[13] Kama Maclean notes in her pioneering book *British India, White Australia* that the early twentieth-century Australian public culture "resonated with enthusiastic support for imperialism."[14] This self-governing "white dominion" strived to present itself as "whiter" than Great Britain.[15] This was often reflected in press stories and columns related to the inter-relations between the two colonies as well as the treatment of Indians in Australia.[16] Despite this fractured relationship, the maritime and trade links between Australia and India mutually permitted many curious and enthusiastic travellers.[17] In the mid-nineteenth century, at the great Intercolonial Exhibition of Australasia held in Melbourne (1866–1867), Australians saw Indian curios, art products, colourful clothing and paintings representing scenes of grand Indian palaces and *bazaars* (markets), along with travelling gipsy dancers from India (Figure 0.2).[18] During these early years of connection, Australians saw only visiting foreign dance and circus companies that performed full-length ballets and a vulgarized form of Hindu temple dance. These companies featured Asian and Indian people as exotic oriental fantasies or freaks. These were shaped heavily by both colonial and anti-colonial discourses and dances made to represent the erotic sensuality and enlightened spirituality of India.[19]

Early Australian representations of Indian culture on stage and in radio productions, as well as in film and music, suffered from the influence of European imperial-colonial representations and the popular religio-culturalist constructs of India that resulted from the varied colonial encounters.[20] Sitara Thobani observes that one of the most recognizable images of the Hindu dancer was of the Hindu dancing girl—*devadasi* and *nautch* girls.[21] Such *nautch* (dance) included aphrodisiacal performances and erotic fantasy to satisfy the needs of spectators.[22] So, Australians who travelled to colonial India as *sahibs* (elite Western visitors) were primarily shown performances by such *nautch* girls—women "performing a shadow of degenerated forms of Kathak"—in North Indian towns.[23] In Europe and the United States of America, the Hindu dance was reborn with white dancers.[24] The oriental dance and arts were mainly composed of exotic

Figure 0.2 A *nautch* dancing girl with a musician (c. 1860); Medium: opaque watercolour and gold paint on paper (Company style); Measurements: 22.1 × 17.8 cm (image and sheet), Place/s of Execution: Patna, Bihar, India.

Source: Accession Number: 2007.520.

Department: Asian Art.

https://www.ngv.vic.gov.au/explore/collection/work/84208/.

Photograph Courtesy: National Gallery of Victoria, Melbourne (Purchased NGV Foundation, 2007. This digital record has been made available on NGV Collection Online through the generous support of The Gordon Darling Foundation) figures, mysterious women, vibrant colours and elaborate temple or court designs.[25]

Joan Erdman argues that the opportunity to promote oriental dance came couched in an environment of curiosity and unfamiliarity.[26] In the 1920s, many influential performers from the West—Anna Pavlova,[27] Ruth St. Denis,[28] Ted Shawn,[29] Sol Hurok,[30] Esther Luella Sherman (aka Ragini Devi),[31] Martha Graham,[32] Jean Erdman,[33] and La Meri[34]—turned to India and Hinduism for inspiration and experimentation (Figure 0.3). Fernau Hall, a well-known dance critic for *The Daily Telegraph*, notes that Indian (Hindu) temple dance made a strong impression on the Western world as early as 700 AD in Spain. The nineteenth-century European ballet choreographers—unlike American choreographers of the twentieth century—were unprepared to incorporate elements of Indian dance into ballet and restricted themselves to suggestive movements.[35] Erdman writes that once oriental dance became a popular

Figure 0.3 Ruth St Denis sitting with a *veena* [an Indian musical string instrument] in her lap, New York, 26 February 1933.

Source: Photographer: Arnold Genthe.

Collection: Arnold Genthe Collection.

https://www.loc.gov/pictures/item/agc1996003199/PP/.

Photograph Courtesy: Library of Congress Prints and Photographs Division Washington, D.C.

genre "created by western devotees with eastern ideas and values," the style influenced dancers in both Europe and the Orient.[36] Furthering this view, Ralph Yarrow observes that many of these practitioners felt something was "missing" or "lacking" from Western art and theatre—something "psychospiritual, technical, aesthetic or a combination of them all."[37] Here, Mary Louise Pratt's notion of the contact zone—"social spaces where cultures meet, clash and grapple with each other, often in contexts of highly asymmetrical relations of power"—becomes pertinent.[38] Like many of her European and American counterparts mentioned, Louise Lightfoot (with her dance partner Mischa Burlakov) decided to recreate Hindu dance pieces for an Australian audience.

Prior to Louise Lightfoot's intervention, Jim Masselos observes that the local "attitudes and approaches" towards Orientalist India were "subsumed within wider processes and developments ostensibly only tangentially about India and more about reinforcing dominant ideas about Australian nationhood."[39] Therefore, most theatrical novelties or ballet works performed in Sydney or Melbourne alluding to Indian settings, stories or characters, were replete with exoticism and stereotypes aimed at Western audiences. Such works included ballets like *The Indian Maid* (1835) and *The Sultan's Choice* (1858), and musical operas *A Moorish Maid* (1905), *The Golden Threshold* (1907), *Cora, the Temptress* (1915) and *The Rajah of Shivapore* (1917)—all "orientalist [spectacles] ready for consumption."[40] In Australian music, some Indian influences and rhythms, a consequence of the universal popularity of the Beatles, became evident particularly in the Jazz works of Bruce Clarke (1963) and Charlie Munro (1967), and the counterculture rock music of The Twilights (1968) and Terry Britten (1968).[41] Introducing Hindu or Indian classical dance as such to this landscape, Louise Lightfoot played a major role in transforming it.[42]

In *The Celestial Dancers: Manipuri Dance on Australian Stage*, I have attempted to chart the extraordinary, historic journey of the popularization of Manipur's Hindu dances in Australia, from 1951 through 1957. Using archival and textual research, newspaper reports, advertisements, programme brochures and Louise's journal entries related to the first Manipuri dancers—Rajkumar Priyagopal Singh, Lakshman Singh and Ibetombi Devi—I have traced their historic Australian tours. I have analyzed how this Hindu dance, a domain of the celestial nymphs and gods, transformed between the temples of Manipur and the stage, and rose up the figure of the North-Eastern Indian cultural guru.[43]

The book is divided into five chapters. As this journey of dance from India to Australia is focused on a Hindu dance form, the first chapter,

"Understanding Hinduism and Vaishnavism," provides a brief history of one of the world's oldest living religions and acquaints the readers with the key ideas governing the use of terms—Hindu and Hinduism. As the Hindu religion and its history are difficult to date and a subject of much scholarly and public debate, I focus on the rise and revival of Hinduism and the emergence of Vaishnavism in Manipur. I argue that the emergence of the *Bhakti* tradition in Hinduism and Vaishnavism in Manipur had a far-reaching impact on society, literature, arts and culture.

In Chapter 2, "The Hindu dances of Manipur," I introduce some key dance forms that comprise Manipuri dance. Manipuri dance is an integral part of the eleven reorganized dance forms compositely categorized as *Bhartiya Shastriya Nritya* (Indian Classical Dance) by the Government of India. This chapter also presents how traditional Hindu dance developed over the centuries with the help of both religious and local cultural practices. It briefly updates the readers on the many institutions revolving around the figure of women dancers; prominently the *devadasis* in South India. The chapter also chronicles the history of folk forms into Manipuri dance, and its development within the rubric of Indian Classical Dance with the help of government funding, which has been interpreted as a political move by the Indian state, to integrate Manipur and its traditions into the dominant culture of India.

In Chapter 3, "The making of an Australian impresario," traces Louise Lightfoot's journey from being a trained architect to becoming a successful ballet teacher and later an impresario for Indian dancers presenting a range of Hindu or Indian classical dance forms around the world. It also presents a brief history and the performances of the Lightfoot-Burlakov school from 1929 to 1937. The highlight of this chapter is Lightfoot's first impression of Uday Shankar's dance in London, which inspired her to move to Bombay and learn Indian classical dance so she could bring greater authenticity to her own ballet. For another five years, Louise lived in Kerala and Tamil Nadu to learn different techniques of the sacred Kathakali and Bharatanatyam dance styles. I briefly recount the performance of the first Hindu artist, renowned Kathakali dancer and teacher Ananda Shivaram, who toured Australia between 1947 and 1949. The chapter concludes with Lightfoot learning of another difficult and intricate dance style from Manipur and her resolve to present it in her own, unique way, to Australians.

Chapter 4, "The prince and his drummer," outlines the journey of two remarkable artists—Rajkumar Priyagopal Singh and Lakshman Singh—who brought Manipuri dance into the international dance arena. The chapter begins with Louise's visit to Bombay in 1951 for a meeting with Manipuri artist Priyagopal to discuss Manipuri dance, his career on the global stage, and future plans. It sketches the history of Priyagopal's family, his dance training, national fame as a performer in major dance centres of India, including Delhi, Calcutta and Bombay (now Kolkata and Mumbai), and explores his ambition to bring Manipuri dance on the world stage. He had won national accolades and was eager to establish himself as a Guru in the international dance circuit, like his contemporaries Uday Shankar and Shivaram, whose careers had been carved and shaped in the West by Anna Pavlova and Louise Lightfoot. The chapter concludes with an acknowledgement of the orientalist gaze which informed Australian public perception viewing his performances, and also of the rift between Priyagopal and Louise which finally ended their dance partnership.

In Chapter 5, "The Goddess of dancing," we return with Louise to Manipur, where she went for a research trip, and completed her book on the local folk and ritual music. From here, Louise was able to introduce another outstanding young dancer on the world stage, Kshetrimayum Ibetombi Devi, an exponent of the pre-Hindu ritualistic priestess dances *Jagoi* and *Maibee* (*Maibi*). It presents how with Louise's support, Ibetombi Devi was able to develop and present her Manipuri (*Meitei*) temple dances as high art. The chapter concludes with Ibetombi Devi's successful Australian tour of 1957, with Shivaram, offering commentary on finance, reputation and cultural understanding.

In the final chapter, I reflect on the challenge faced by the two pioneering Manipuri dancers, to experiment with the age-old tradition and present their art on the Australian stage. Louise, Rajkumar Priyagopal Singh, and Ibetombi Devi's success in experimenting and promoting Manipur's Hindu dance forms was an uncommon one and bears careful study as a collaborative process.

This book tells the story of the making of renowned Indian exponents and cultural gurus who took Manipuri dance forms to the global stage. Eminent critics of Indian dance have argued that such international exposure added substantially to the dignity of both the dance and the dancers, especially as they emerged from under long European domination and humiliation. Post-1957, many more renowned Manipuri dancers have made their impact on the global stage. However, given the scope of this book, I have kept to discussing the contribution of Rajkumar Priyagopal Singh and Ibetombi Devi in popularizing and presenting Manipuri dance in Australia. I hope that their story will prompt further research and publication on Hindu dance and Australia-India contemporary dance connections.

Notes

1 For a discussion, see Niyogi-Nakra, "Indian Dance outside India," 309–315; O'Shea, *At Home in the World*, 2007; Chakravorty and Gupta, eds. *Dance Matters*, 2012; Sarwal, *The Dancing God*, 2020.
2 Davis, "A Shared History?" 849–869.
3 For a discussion on Australian perceptions of India, see Hosking and Sarwal, *Wanderings in India*, 2012; Walker and Sobocinska, *Australia's Asia*, 2012; Walker, "National Narratives," 2002; Walker, *Experiencing Turbulence*, 2013; Walker, *Stranded Nation*, 2019.
4 For a discussion on educated Indians' views on Australia, see Allen, "Observing Australia as the 'Member of an Alien and Conquered Race'," 2009a; Allen, "Otim Singh in White Australia," 2009b; Allen, "Identifying Sher Mohamad," 2013; De Lepervanche, *Indians in a White Australia*, 1984; Maclean, "India in Australia," 2012; Maclean, *British India, White Australia*, 2020.
5 Bennett et al., eds, *Of Sadhus and Spinners*, 2009; Zubrzycki, *Jadoowallahs, Jugglers and Jinns*, 2018 (this book was first published as *Empire of Enchantment: The Story of Indian Magic* by Scribe).
6 Sarwal, *South Asian Diaspora Narratives*, 2016.
7 The Afghans or Ghans were cameleers who worked in Australian outback from the 1860s to 1930s. See "Afghan cameleers in Australia," 2009; Rajkowski, *In the Tracks of the Camelmen*, 1987; Khatun, *Australianama*, 2018.
8 Refer to Earnshaw, "Lang, John (1816–1864)," 1974; Medcalf, "John Lang, Our Forgotten Indian Envoy," 2010.
9 Darwin, *Unfinished Empire*, 2012.
10 On James Inglis, see Rutledge, "Inglis, James (1845–1908)," 1972; Walker, *Anxious Nation*, 1999.
11 Zubrzycki, *The Last Nizam*, 2006.
12 For a discussion on colonial connections between Australia and India, see Walker, *Anxious Nation*, 1999; Westrip and Holroyde, *Colonial Cousins*, 2010; Bayly, "India and Australia," 2012.
13 Refer to Ahmed, "India's Membership of the Commonwealth – Nehru's Role," 1991; Walker, *Anxious Nation*, 1999; Broinowski, *About Face*, 2003; Bayly, "India and Australia," 2012.
14 Maclean, *British India, White Australia*, 2.
15 See Heath, *Purifying Empire*, 3; Maclean, *British India, White Australia*, 2–3.
16 Maclean, *British India, White Australia*, 135–163.
17 For a discussion on various travellers, see Bilimoria, "Speaking of the Hindu Diaspora in Australia," 1998; Allen, "'Innocents Abroad' and 'Prohibited Immigrants'," 2005; Allen, "'A Fine Type of Hindoo' meets 'the Australian Type'," 2008.
18 Through the Intercolonial Exhibition (24 October 1866 to 23 February 1867) the Australian colonies came together for the first time. See "Melbourne: Intercolonial Exhibition of Australasia 1866-67," 2017.
19 Thobani, *Indian Classical Dance and the Making of Postcolonial National Identities*, 147.
20 For a discussion on the influence of European imperial-colonial representations, see Scott-Maxwell, "Asia and Pacific Links," 54; Broinowski, *The Yellow Lady*, 1996; Walker, *Anxious Nation*, 1999; Bilimoria, "Indian Dance," 2003; Bilimoria, "The Spiritual Transformation of Indian Dance in Australia," 2008; Thobani, *Indian Classical Dance and the Making of Postcolonial National Identities*, 147.

21 Thobani, *Indian Classical Dance and the Making of Postcolonial National Identities*, 2017.
22 Hanna, *Dance, Sex, and Gender*, 1988.
23 Coorlawala, "Ruth St. Denis and India's Dance Renaissance," 130.
24 Srinivasan, *Sweating Saris*, 63–64.
25 Erdman, "Dance Discourses," 1996.
26 Ibid.
27 Anna Pavlova was a well-known Russian prima ballerina of the Imperial Russian Ballet and the Ballets Russes in the late 19th and the early 20th centuries. See Dandré, *Anna Pavlova*, 1932/1979; Sorell, *Dance in its Time*, 1986.
28 Ruth St. Denis was an American contemporary dance innovator who studied Hindu dance, art and philosophy. In her tours, she added *The Nautch* and *The Yogi* to her dance program. See Desmond, "Dancing out the Difference," 256–270.
29 Ted Shawn (Edwin Myers Shawn) was a pioneer of American modern dance. He was the creator of Denishawn and "The Cosmic Dance of Shiva." See Terry, *Ted Shawn*, 1976.
30 Sol Hurok was a 20th-century American dance impresario who managed well-known performing artists. See Robinson, *The Last Impresario*, 1994.
31 Ragini Devi made her impact on Indian classical dance and stage even before Rukmini Devi and Sri Vallathol. See Devi, *Dance Dialects of India*, 1990; Rahman, *Dancing in the Family*, 2002; Sen, "Return of the Prodigy," 1976.
32 Martha Graham was an American modern dancer and choreographer best known for her style—the 'Graham technique.' See Horosko, *Martha Graham*, 2002.
33 Jean Erdman is an American dancer, choreographer and theatre director.
34 La Meri was an American dancer, choreographer, teacher, poet, anthropologist, and scholar. In the 1930s, La Meri invited Indian classical dance guru Ram Gopal to tour with her extensively in the West. See Au and Rutter, *Ballet and Modern Dance*, 2012.
35 For a discussion on incorporation of elements of Indian dance into ballet, see Hall, "The Contribution of Indian Dance to British Culture," 1982; Bilimoria, "Traditions and Transition in South Asian Performing Arts in Multicultural Australia," 115.
36 Erdman, "Dance Discourses," 1996.
37 Yarrow, *Indian Theatre*, 16.
38 Pratt, "Arts of the Contact Zone," 34.
39 Masselos, "Two Places and Three Times," 133.
40 Srinivasan, *Sweating Saris*, 142.
41 For a detailed discussion on exoticism and stereotypes, see Broinowski, *The Yellow Lady*, 1996; Walker, *Anxious Nation*, 1999; Scott-Maxwell, "Asia and Pacific Links," 2003; Bilimoria, "Indian Dance," 330–331.
42 Masselos, "Two Places and Three Times," 136.
43 Mary Louise Lightfoot published an account of Louise's visit to India in a beautiful book entitled *Lightfoot Dancing: An Australian-Indian Affair* (2015).

1 Understanding Hinduism and Vaishnavism[1]

The "Hindu temple dance" or dances associated with the Hindu temple tradition were reborn in Europe and the United States with pre-dominantly "white dancers" performing and transforming religious rituals.[2] Manipur's *Meitei* and *Vaishnava* dances too were first introduced to the global stage contextualized as traditional temple dancing—and referred to as "Hindu dance."[3] Lightfoot's own dance group in Australia was named the Hindu Dance Group, and as an impresario, Louise's interest was in presenting "authentic Hindu culture and art" to the Australian audience.[4] As prelude to history, politics and religion in Manipur, this chapter dwells on the nuances of being a Hindu, of Hinduism, Vaishnavism, and the interrelationship between religion and dance as art in India.

The words Hindu, Hinduism and Hindutva have become variously charged over the past several years and have become a recurrent topic of fraught discussion in a variety of fora, both in India and abroad. Without getting caught up in the controversies surrounding the recent debates on Hindutva, a term that has since the 1990s been widely used as a marker for the resurgence of Hindu nationalism in India,[5] let us start with the idea of the Hindu, and of Hinduism.[6]

Scholars specializing in the history of the Hindu religion and its traditions claim it is the "world's oldest religion" based on textual evidence from the *Rig Veda*.[7] The knotty question of whether Hindu religious traditions arose in the Indus Valley, 3300–1300 BCE, or whether they came with the Vedic Aryans is directly pertinent to developing an understanding of how, much later, Hinduism came to and was established in Manipur.[8] There are two major theories: the Aryan Invasion theory and the Cultural Transformation theory. According to the first theory, the Aryans invaded and their religious texts—the *Vedas*—became dominant in the Indian sub-continent. The second theory interprets Aryan culture and its sacred texts as part of the development narrative of

DOI: 10.4324/9781003205203-2

the Indus Valley civilization.[9] The commonest argument goes that since Hindus did not believe in the linearity of time before colonialism imposed it as an organizational construct on them, exact dates of Hinduism's development are unavailable. However, periods of their history have been logically inferred from textual references. Hinduism has existed in India, as a belief system and an unbroken intellectual tradition, for three thousand years. Unlike the Abrahamic religions, Hinduism is not a single religion but embraces many ancient traditions and philosophies, going back even longer. In fact, it is "no religion" in the Abrahamic sense. There is no single reference book to practice the belief systems, which are diverse and often contradict one another. The word *dharma* as used by Hindus refers not merely to religious or spiritual practice but also ethical daily living and denotes righteousness of thought and action.

Scottish historian and philosopher James Mill, in *The History of British India,* distinguished three phases in the history of India: Hindu, Muslim and British civilisations.[10] This was of course a very simplistic division of a problematic timeline. The following timeline presents a brief but still more elaborate and accurate chronology of the development of Hinduism in India:

- Up to 2000 BCE: The Indus Valley civilisation
- 1500–500 BCE: The Vedic period
- 500 BCE to 500 CE: The Epics, Puranic and Classical age
- 500–1500 CE: Medieval period and the Islamic Invasion
- 1500–1757 CE: Pre-Modern period and Bhakti movement
- 1757–1947 CE: British period, Hindu renaissance and the emergence of Hindutva ideology
- 1947 CE to the present: Independent India and Hindutva ideology in politics

In her book *Imagining Hinduism*, Sharada Sugirtharajah has argued that Hinduism has been a central reference point in "Western consciousness" and has been defined mostly via "Western categories."[11] Historians Romila Thapar and Arvind Sharma have both noted scholarly attempts made to trace a correspondence between theories of India's (Hindu) past and Biblical ones that have consistently framed it also as Hindu–Muslim polarity.[12] In 1799, for instance, Welsh orientalist William Jones pointed to the close resemblance between the classical languages of Europe and Sanskrit. He declared that the four Hindu *yugas* (ages)—*Satya* or *Krita*, *Treta*, *Dvapara* and *Kali*—have an affinity with Roman and Grecian ages, and those deriving from them. He placed the idea of Hindu *yugas* within a Biblical framework based on common or similar theistic practices. Jones observed:

> We may here observe, that the true History of the World seems obviously divisible into four ages or periods; which may be called, the first, the *Diluvian*, or purest age; namely the times preceding the deluge… next, the *Patriarchal*, or pure age; in which, indeed, there were mighty hunters of beasts and men, …—Thirdly, the *Mosaick*, or less pure age; from the legation of Moses, and during this time when his ordinances were comparatively well observed and uncorrupted—Lastly, the *Prophetical*, or impure age; beginning with the vehement warnings given by the Prophets to apostate Kings and degenerate nations, but still subsiding and to subsist, until all genuine prophecies shall be fully accomplished.[13]

Nevertheless for Jones, through a Biblical lens Hinduism was an "erroneous religion" which had more to do with imagination than reason.[14]

Given this multiplicity of interpretations, are Hindu and Hinduism misleading terms? Hinduism, the religion, is in fact a tradition that encompasses various ideas—from the Vedic to present-day thoughts and values. The Vedic period, which was from 1500 to 500 BCE, is now known for the composition of the ritual texts, epics, *Sutras*, the *Brahmanas*, the *Aranyakas*, *Upanishads* and chiefly the four *Vedas*—the *Rig Veda*, the *Samaveda*, *Yajurveda* and the *Atharvaveda*. But the term "Hindu," post-Vedic period, originally comes from the Sanskrit word "Sindhu" (Sindhu River or Indus River) the region of the cultures of the Indus Valley civilisation (2500–1500 BCE).[15] These people, in some ways, may have been related to the Dravidians in South India but the point is debatable, as the script and writing have yet to be deciphered.[16] In *The Sacred Thread,* J. Brockington comments: "it must not be forgotten that the religion of the Vedas was an alien culture brought into India by the Aryans."[17] The controversial theory of an Aryan presence in India before the Indus Valley Civilisation has not been fully validated and has been debunked by some scholars and historians.[18] In fact, in 1914, Sri Aurobindo discredited this theory by pointing to the exaggerated, overstated and superficial claims made in the nineteenth century by comparative philologists in favour of the linguistic commonality between the Aryan tongue and the Sanskrit language. He observed:

> The first error committed by the philologists after their momentous discovery of the Sanskrit tongue, was to exaggerate the importance of their first superficial discoveries. The first glance is apt to be

superficial; the perceptions drawn from an initial survey stand always in need of correction. If then we are so dazzled and led away by them as to make them the very key of our future knowledge, its central plank, its basic platform we prepare ourselves grievous disappointments. Comparative Philology, guilty of this error, has seized on a minor clue and mistaken it for a major or chief clue.[19]

Debate continues on the myths of origins of India and Hinduism, particularly about the extent of fusion of Aryan and Dravidian traditions. In her article "The Theory of Aryan Race and India," Thapar has shown how Aryan theory began as an attempt to uncover the beginnings of Indian history and explain the society's mythical origins.[20] By using it as a framework, the roots of an Indian identity were established and later used in Hindutva politics.[21] Upper-caste Hindus have used the Aryan lineage theory to prove their own superiority to the indigenous populations of India and equality with the Europeans. Scholars belonging to or sympathising with the lower castes in India and abroad have used it to provide "the Dalit version of history."[22]

Scholars of Hinduism have also argued elsewhere that the term "Hindu" was mostly used by Persians or Muslim conquerors to refer to the inhabitants of the areas near the Indus River and not to any religious denomination. According to A. V. Williams Jackson, the earliest known use of the word "Hindu" appears in the sacred book of Zoroastrianism—*Zend Avesta*:

> The first chapter of the Avestan Vendidad (whatever may be the age of the chapter) contains an allusion to a portion of Northern India in a list which it gives of sixteen lands or regions, created by Ahur Mazda and apparently regarded as under Iranian sway. The fifteenth of these domains, according to Vd. 1, 18 was Hapta Hindu, "Seven Rivers," a region of "abnormal heat," probably identical with the territory of Sapta Sindhavas, "Seven Rivers," in the Veda.
>
> (see especially Rv. VIII, 24, 27)[23]

With travellers coming from Greece, China and Arabia, Sindhu (or Sindh) became "India," "Indu" and "al-Hind," thus acquiring territorial and religious references, respectively.[24] But this idea of India was still confined to Sindh (North). Further, under prevalent definitions in Indian philosophy, being a Hindu was not a way of religious thinking but a way of life.[25] Aziz Ahmad has also pointed to the significance of the Arab conquest of Sind in c.712 and its impact on creating this idea of Hindus as a category for both religious and administrative purposes:

The conquest of Sind by Muhammad ibn Qasim, and the incorporation of that province into the Muslim universal caliphate, brought the Muslims there in a relationship of a very different nature, that of the ruled and the ruler. This form of political relationship, which some centuries later extended to the whole sub-continent, and survived until well into the eighteenth century inevitably led to the creation of tensions which determined very largely the psychological course of the history of medieval and modern India.[26]

The conquest brought about the acceptance and borrowing of the victor's language. This India, in the intriguing words of famous scholar and traveller Alberuni (Al-Biruni), was a religious antagonist of Islam.[27] Alberuni writes:

> Another circumstance which increased the already existing antagonism between Hindus and foreigners is that the so-called Shamaniyya (Buddhists), though they cordially hate Brahmans, still are nearer akin to them than to others. In former times, Khurdsdn, Persis, Irak, Mosul, the country up to the frontier of Syria, was Buddhistic, but then Zarathustra went forth from Adharbaijan and preached Magism in Balkh (Baktra). His doctrine came into favour with King Gushtasp, and his son Isfendiyad spread the new faith both in east and west, both by force and by treaties. He founded fire-temples through his whole empire, from the frontiers of China to those of the Greek empire. The succeeding kings made their religion (i.e., Zoroastrianism) the obligatory state-religion for Persis and Irak. In consequence, the Buddhists were banished from those countries and had to emigrate to the countries east of Balk.[28]

Richard H. Davis has described Alberuni's account of India and Hindus as moving between a centralist (based on the hegemony of Sanskrit texts and Vedic mythology) and a pluralist (tolerance and incorporation of all ideas) approach to Hinduism.[29] Hindus through various sects—*Shaiva* (followers of Shiva), *Vaishnava* (followers of Vishnu), *Shakta* (followers of Devi) and *Smarta* (followers of Brahman and all major deities)—believe that all the deities are a manifestation of one. Eminent Sanskrit scholar J. A. B. van Buitenen, in the *Encyclopedia Britannica*, defined Hinduism in the context of its pluralistic ideals:

> In principle, Hinduism incorporates all forms of belief and worship without necessitating the selection or elimination of any. The

Hindu is inclined to revere the divinity in every manifestation, whatever it may be, and is doctrinally tolerant ... Hinduism is, then, both a civilization and a conglomeration of religions, with neither a beginning, a founder, nor a central authority, hierarchy, or organization.[30]

By the thirteenth century, the word Hindu gave rise to another word—Hindustan. This literally meant "the land of the Hindus" and became synonymous with North India.[31] Here, the amalgamation of all religions—Islam, Buddhism, Sikhism and Sufism—influenced North Indian culture. On the other hand, the original Vedic traditions remained well-preserved in South and some parts of North East India.

Thapar writes that it was only by the fifteenth and sixteenth centuries that the word "Hindu" was formally appropriated by Hindus themselves. This happened under the influence of the *Bhakti* (theistic devotional) movement, to distinguish the Hindu community from the Muslim.[32] Orientalist scholars such as H. H. Wilson, M. Monier-Williams and G. A. Grierson compared *Bhakti* to a monotheistic reform movement, almost at the level of Protestant Christianity, particularly with its focus on one god—Bhagwan Vishnu—and its criticism of caste.[33] There are many images and interpretations of the *Bhakti* movement as it works on a complex structure of complex participation.[34] Hinduism, with the emergence of *Bhakti* tradition and its sub-religion Vaishnavism that was chiefly devoted to Bhagwan Vishnu and his incarnation Bhagwan Shri Krishna had in fact a far-reaching impact on Manipuri society, literature, art and dance. Vaishnavism became the recognized religion of the Manipuris, and according to Saryu Doshi, "merged diverse philosophical and cultural elements" to inspire a number of folk, temple and classical dance forms.[35] Vaishnavism is one of the oldest religions of India. As a religion, it is based on the philosophies outlined in the *Upanishads*, *Vedanta Sutras* and the *Bhagwad-Gita*.[36] Some of its main features are: it is strictly monotheistic system that upholds Bhagwan Vishnu (and his *avatars*) as the ultimate reality (*paratattva*) and teaches that devotion to Bhagwan Vishnu leads one to the realization of one's ultimate goal (*parampurussharaartha*); it proposes *Bhakti* as the only way to attain salvation (*moksha*); it advocates the practice of non-violence (*ahimsa*) towards every living creature; and enjoyment of the natural (*svabhavika*) and unconditional (*nirhetuka*) grace of God (*anuraag*) as the ultimate goal of life.[37]

In the seventeenth century, Hinduism travelled to remote regions of North East India as an influential tool of social reformation and made many local kings abandon their faith and gods by recontextualising ancient Vedic traditions.[38] Prior to this, ancient Manipur had been known to kingdoms surrounding it by names such as *Meitrabak*, *Kangleipak* or *Meeteileipak*.[39] Some ancient Manipuri texts and narratives based on myths and legends of the land reflect the spatial and cosmic imagination of the people. Thingnam Sanjeev points to some important texts, such as *Lammitlon*, *Poireiton Kunthok*, *Panthoibi Khongul* and *Leihou Naofamlol*, which deal with the *Meiteis'* migration or movement, perception of their landscape, the process of naming the land and their deep ritual connections to the earth.[40] Lokendro Arambam, in his preface to *Lammitlon*, argues that the geography of Manipur made it possible for the *Meitei* community to develop a network of signs, communication, symbols and belief system to create acceptance of the land.[41] Through language and ritual practices, Sanjeev argues, Manipur was marked and its identity validated to create a sense of belongingness for *Meiteis*.[42]

Other Medieval era Manipuri manuscripts also evidence that Hindus from the mainland Indian sub-continent were married to Manipur royalty.[43] However, the turning point in Manipur's history was the installation of the image of Bhagwan Vishnu in a temple at Lamangdong by King Meidingu Senbi Kiyamba (1467–1508). This marked the advent of Vaishnavism in Manipur. King Kiyamba's son Meidingu Khagemba (1597–1652), on the other hand, favoured *Meitei* religious practices and literature.[44] With later rulers began the transition period from traditional *Meitei* culture to a full Hinduisation of the majority of *Meitei* society, especially via the building of Hindu temples in the region.

According to N. Lokendra Singh, three Vaishnavite sects, Nimandi, Ramandi and Chaitanya Vaishnavism, also entered Manipur along with Hinduism in the late seventeenth and early eighteenth centuries.[45] These sects, products of the *Bhakti* movement, arose against the rigidity of Hinduism.[46] While Nimandi led by Nimbaraka promoted the worship of Krishna and Krishnaa, Ramandi led by Ramananda preached the worship of Rama and Sita in the vernacular language. The third and most popular sect, Chaitanya Vaishnavism, on the other hand, opposed the religious rituals, Brahamanical rites and caste-related ceremonies. Its leader Chaitanya preached brotherhood and love for all (Hindus and Muslims alike) through the worship of Radha and Krishna. This sect had a greater influence on *Meiteis* as it reflected a progressive ideology.[47]

So, in the eighteenth century, during the reign of King Meidingu Pamheiba (Garibniwaz, 1709–1748), the Chaitanya Vaishnavism school of Hinduism was declared the state religion. Consequently, the Vaishnavism of Chaitanya Mahaprabhu took deep root. Sohini Ray argues that this radical change brought both "marginalisation" and "ethnic disparity" into Manipur society by introducing the caste system and dominance of Brahmins.[48] On the other hand, Sruti Bandopadhay observes that Vaishnavism brought the much needed unification of Manipuri social life.[49] Vaishnava worship was expressed through an aesthetic of romantic love for the divine, especially in the royal court of Manipur. The translation of Hindu epics and religious texts and the use of Bengali and Sanskrit scripts was encouraged, over local *Meitei* scripts and manuscripts. The Sanskrit epics, the *Mahabharata* and *Ramayana,* were translated into *Meitei* and many other Sanskrit *parvas* were written by Angom Gopi, renowned scholar and poet at the court of Pamheiba. Hinduism reached its peak during the reign of King Meidingu Chingthang Khomba (aka Rajarshi Bhagyachandra or Jai Singh Maharaja, 1748–1799; Figure 1.1). He acquired fame for introducing *Ras Lila,* the highest spiritual expression of worshipping Bhagwan Krishna, in dance form. He was an ardent devotee of Chaitanya Mahaprabhu and a statue of Nityananda was installed during his reign. Hinduism became the religion of the majority, with a minority practicing *Sanamahism,* the traditional *Meitei* religion.[50] In 1859, W. McCulloch observed that the hold of Hinduism as a new religion among the *Meiteis* was superficial—"a religion professed, not from conviction, but because it is a fashion."[51] He observes that the way Manipur's local population accepts Hinduism shows that "their observations are only for appearance sake, not the promptings of the heart."[52] However, by the end of the eighteenth century, Hinduism's customs and practices were solidified by subsequent kings as a mark of shared religiosity, often protested by *Meiteis,* who considered the religion

Figure 1.1 A portrait of Meitei monarch King Rajarshi Bhagyachandra (1748–1799).

Source: Photograph: India Post, Government of India.

Public Domain.

Photograph Courtesy: https://commons.wikimedia.org/wiki/File:Ching-Thang_Khomba_2000_stamp_of_India.jpg.

an intrusion that had destroyed traditional religion, identity, culture and ways of life.[53] Arambam explains that in pre-colonial Manipur, ritualistic performances were the main basis of statecraft. He argues that the *Meiteis* practised the control of territorial administrative arrangement through Hindu rites and rituals.[54]

With the coming of the British, the word Hindu began to be used as an umbrella term "to characterize all things in India."[55] Wilfred Cantwell Smith, in *Meaning and End of Religion*, has also observed that the use of the word Hindu in the meaning "Indian" survived in popular English into the twentieth century.[56] The term Hindu in the eighteenth and nineteenth centuries came to be associated predominantly with a religious identity among people in India, such as Christian and Muslim, by British administrators. In this context, Sugirtharajah observes that it was the "Orientalists" who categorized and compartmentalized India, Hinduism, the sacred texts and the Sanskrit language. She writes:

> Orientalists saw themselves as "discovering" India's ancient past and as enlightening the Hindu elite with their newly discovered knowledge. Orientalists, in studying the ancient Sanskrit texts, came to textualize, restructure, and domesticate them.[57]

Among Hindus, the Young Bengal Group in 1840s Calcutta (now Kolkata) saw itself as a collection of reformers and spoke of Hindus and Hinduism critically. For these Hindu reformers, a purified Hinduism meant a socio-religious practice that can correspond to universal va-lues.[58] By the end of the nineteenth century, Indian modernists such as Raja Rammohan Roy, Sri Aurobindo and Swami Vivekananda,[59] were helping purify Hinduism by elevating the Vedic elements and framing the global appeal of its philosophies.[60]

It was only in the twentieth century that the term Hindu was re-constructed and associated with the emergence of Hindutva as a political force and a source of national identity in India. It can be argued that neo-Vedanta indirectly contributed to the Hindutva ideology and politics. Even Mahatma Gandhi, leader of the Indian National Congress (INC), called himself a *Sanatani* Hindu because of his strong belief in the *Vedas*, the *Upanishads*, the *Puranas* the *Varanshrama Dharma* and the protection of the cow (Figure 1.2).[61] In the 1920s, Gandhi focussed on Hinduism, not as an exclusive or a missionary religion but as one which was all-encompassing and peaceful. In an article published in *Young India*, he wrote:

> Believing as I do in the influence of heredity, being born in a Hindu family, I have remained a Hindu. I should reject it, if I found

Figure 1.2 Mahatma Gandhi with Kasturba on their return to India from South Africa, in 1915.

Source: Photograph: Press Information Bureau, Government of India.

https://digicoll.manoa.hawaii.edu.

Photograph Courtesy: Gandhi Photos (1886–1948), University of Hawai'i.

it inconsistent with my moral sense or my spiritual growth. On examination, I have found it to be the most tolerant of all religions known to me. Its freedom from dogma makes a forcible appeal to me inasmuch as it gives the votary the largest scope for self-expression. Not being an exclusive religion, it enables the followers of that faith not merely to respect all the other religions, but it also enables them to admire and assimilate whatever may be good in the other faiths. Non-violence is common to all religions, but it has found the highest expression and application in Hinduism. (I do not regard Jainism or Buddhism as separate from Hinduism.) Hinduism believes in the oneness not of merely all human life but in the oneness of all that lives. Its worship of the cow is, in my opinion, its unique contribution to the evolution of humanitarianism. It is a practical application of the belief in the oneness and, therefore, sacredness, of all life. The great belief in transmigration is a direct consequence of that belief. Finally, the discovery of the law of *Varnashrama* is a magnificent result of the ceaseless search for truth.[62]

Some believed that there was an ambiguity in Gandhi's "soft Hindutva" that resulted in communal conflicts and dissatisfaction among Muslims and Dalits from the 1920s onwards. David Page, discussing the communal conflict of the 1920s, observes how the political reforms of 1919 "gave way to communal antagonism."[63] Many Congress workers and leaders, in the 1930s and 1940s, identified with the idea of a "Hindu nation," based on the fluidity of the term as applied to a secular nation for all.[64] This idea was subsequently promoted by Gandhi's contemporary, Vinayak Damodar Savarkar, in a different form: based on a form of militant, exclusionary and exclusive Hinduism (Figure 1.3).

Savarkar believed that competition between Hindu and Muslim communities served as the basis for hatred and that this divisiveness could be cured if and only if Indians were able to identify themselves as "Hindu" or there was a provision for two states in the sub-continent—Hindu and Muslim.[65] Savarkar popularized the term Hindutva (Hinduness) in his 1923 pamphlet entitled *Hindutva: Who is a Hindu?*[66] His work was published at a time when Indian nationalism and the independence movement was in their heyday; Hindutva was promoted as nationalized monotheistic Hinduism or the promotion of a "Hindu Rashtra"

Figure 1.3 A portrait of Vinayak Damodar "Veer" Savarkar.

Source: Public Domain.

Photograph Courtesy: Swatantryaveer Savarkar Rashtriya Smarak (Mumbai, India).

(a Hindu nation), based largely on western Christian political theologies of dominion, tied together by blood, consciousness and ancient land.[67] Savarkar writes:

> We Hindus are bound together not only by the tie of the love we bear to a common fatherland and by the common blood that courses through our veins and keeps our hearts throbbing and our affections warm, but also by the tie of the common homage we pay to our great civilization—our Hindu culture.[68]

Being Hindu (the religion) and adhering to Hindutva (the ideology) were two different things, however. Hinduism was a religion with many sub-sects, belief systems and traditions and Savarkar's idea of Hindutva was based on a political and nationalistic ideology identifying all Indians, regardless of their religious identities, as "Hindus" as a geographical construct, referring to a unifying geographical boundary.

In his pamphlet, Savarkar approached the question through both the religious and the historical lens, focusing on people living in the Indian sub-continent as Hindu people with one ethnic, cultural and political identity. Janaki Bakhle places Savarkar among the four most important anticolonial nationalists along with Mahatma Gandhi, Pundit Jawaharlal Nehru and Netaji Subhas Chandra Bose.[69] His political ideology of Hindutva, as has been noted by Sumanta Banerjee, was based on a combination of received tradition, history and mythology and an active refashioning of this tradition, modulated to legitimize the exercise of authority.[70] This model was based on objectively authoritarian inferences and didn't actually address India's social, cultural and economic conflicts.[71] Ashis Nandy has observed that Savarkar's ideology influenced sections of urban, middle-class, modernizing Hindus of British India.[72] Nandy observes that Savarkar himself was influenced by Brahmabandhav Upadhyay, a Catholic theologian, Vedantic scholar and a pioneer in indigenous Christian theology.[73] Upadhyay was also a Hindu nationalist scholar-activist whose political Hinduism finally ended up as Savarkar's Hindutva.[74] In the 1940s, the Muslim League leader Mohammad Ali Jinnah proposed his two-nation theory based on the Hindu–Muslim divide. Savarkar declared on August 15, 1943: "I have no quarrel with Mr Jinnah's two-nation theory. We Hindus are a nation by ourselves and it is a historical fact that Hindus and Muslims are two nations."[75] But post-independence, Savarkar's life became controversial because of his role in Mahatma Gandhi's murder and his letters promising loyalty to the British authorities.[76] The glorification of Savarkar's ideology by the Rashtriya Swayamsevak Sangh (RSS; formed in the 1920s), the

Vishwa Hindu Parishad (VHP; formed in the 1960s), the Shiv Sena (formed in the 1960s) and the Bharatiya Janata Party (BJP; formed in the 1970s) facilitate the internalization of the political force of Hindu Indian nationalism.[77] For these religious-political groups, the philosophy of Hindutva signifies a supposedly common agreement on Hindu identity which leaves no room for any other way of life or belief system, such as those of Muslims or Christians.[78]

Today, Savarkar's ideology of Hindutva has attained legitimacy in India, the world's largest secular democracy, and Manipur is no exception to this transactional politics as a majority of the *Meitei* population comprises of Hindus.[79] Critics label the winning of state elections by the BJP as the rise of "Hindu fundamentalism" in Manipur.[80] However, in the last decade, BJP has moved steadily forward in northeastern states through regional political alliances, using secular candidates and carefully managing solutions for controversial issues. This also includes recent promises such as documenting and archiving indigenous cultural and traditional art forms, creating Manipuri Study Centers at premier universities, establishing cultural complexes for performing arts, and launching artists pension scheme.[81] These promises accompany less savoury agendas such as anti-conversion bills and selling to sympathetic ears its ideology of *Akhand Bharat* (Undivided India or Greater India), an India that is united by its *vedic* and Sanskritic cultural roots.[82] Also, given India's political landscape and normalized ideological mimicking by national and regional level parties across the board, I do not agree with oversimplified definitions of "Hindu communalism" or "Hindu fundamentalism." It is apparent that, with the changing political landscape, notions drawn from Congress' "soft Hindutva" of the 1930s and 1940s are being re-employed as a strategy for cultivating political currency.[83] Two events, the visit of Congress President Rahul Gandhi to almost all popular Hindu temples to prove his identity as a "Hindu" and the publication of *Why I Am a Hindu* by senior Congress leader and well-known author Shashi Tharoor, have demonstrated the ease with which the Congress can appeal for and persuade votes through its own brand of "soft Hindutva." The Congress and neoliberal voters articulate a "Hinduism" (plural and tolerant) versus "Hindutva" (singular and intolerant) narrative. However, all hard and soft Hindutva movements are anchored in so-called historical grievances and discord and seek solutions in their own ways to redress them. I argue that any study of Hindu communalism, or fundamentalism or nationalism in India, must begin with the role of individual politicians, across parties, manipulating religious rhetoric.[84]

From the late nineteenth century onwards, as William Gould notes, "the gears of communal conflict" in India are often "lubricated by competition over social and political resources, rather than the deliberate manipulation of religious symbols."[85] The "Hindu nationalist" ideology of the BJP, for instance, has more to do with politics than a spiritually enriched, tolerant and adaptable religion. Once in office, the BJP-led government implemented several of the traditionally authoritarian promises of its Hindu nationalist programme, especially rewriting of history books, changing names of places deemed colonial or offensive to Hindus and banning cow slaughter (except where relevant to India's beef export crop). Overall, it has also involved itself in populist projects ostensibly aimed at national unity, the fight against corruption, infrastructure development, ease of doing business and the fight against terrorism. Several leaders have damaged outright the spirit of Hinduism by indulging in tirades against minorities, especially when they have framed "Hinduism" as inherently oppositional to the Abrahamic religions. However, given the continuities in and discrepancies fostered by Hindu nationalism, and the fairly systematic resistance mounted by Dalit and Muslim activists, the Hindutva movement's dream of reshaping Indian society in its own image is a far-fetched one. As Avijit Pathak points out, the inherent ethos of Hinduism is inclusivity:

> Its epics constantly remind me of the dharma of life, the interplay of good and evil, the dynamics of *tamas*, *rajas* and *sattva*, and the riddle of human existence. Its Upanishads take me to the realm of sublime prayers: a longing for the transcendental—the way Rabindranath Tagore composed his enchanting songs.
>
> Likewise, sages like Ramakrishna and Raman Maharshi arouse meditative calmness, love and ecstasy, and the likes of Vivekananda and Gandhi inspire us to unite the three yogas—love, knowledge and action. With this tradition of Hinduism, all the walls of separation are broken. Gautam Buddha and Narayan Guru, Surdas and Mira, Nizamuddin Auliya and Mother Teresa, Tagore and Nehru, and Lokayat and Vedanta: nothing is alien; it is an ocean that absorbs everything.[86]

The definition of India as an ocean or a space for plurality, peace and regard for multiple traditions is important. This space, according to Makarand R. Paranjape, offers an alternative to conquest and socially damaging categorization.[87] As political change is still unfolding, tracing and understanding the growth of Hindu nationalism from the early days of the Hindu renaissance to the present does not suggest that India's linguistic, cultural, religious, artistic, intellectual, social and political diversity will allow any political party to shape this secular nation into a Hindu nation state.[88]

Notes

1 I am grateful to my friend Prof. Dhananjay Singh, Centre for English Studies at Jawaharlal Nehru University, for his insightful comments and timely feedback on this chapter. Parts of this chapter have appeared as "Hindu, Hinduism and Hindutva" in *The Dancing God: Staging Hindu Dance in Australia* (2020). Published here with the permission of Routledge.
2 Srinivasan, *Sweating Saris*, 63–64.
3 There is no official category called "Hindu dance" in India. Post-independence, the dances were collectively referred to as *Bhartiya shastriya nritya* (Indian Classical Dance). A discussion on this topic will follow in Chapter 2 of this book.
4 Lightfoot, *Lightfoot Dancing*, 2015.
5 For a discussion on the genealogical study of Hindu right-wing nationalism, see Banerjee, "'Hindutva': Ideology and Social Psychology," 1991; Basu, *Hindutva as Political Monotheism*, 2020.
6 For a discussion on Hinduism's origins, key philosophical concepts, criticism of politicized Hinduism and its re-examination, see Tharoor, *Why I Am a Hindu*, 2018.
7 For a discussion on the history of the Hindu religion and tradition, see Flood, *An Introduction to Hinduism*, 1996; Fowler, *Hinduism: Beliefs and Practices*, 1997; Lorenzen, "Who Invented Hinduism?" 1999; Klostermaier, *A Survey of Hinduism*, 2007; Whaling, *Understanding Hinduism*, 2009.
8 It is also a matter of debate whether the "Aryan invasion," as it is referred to by a school of historians, indeed took place.
9 For a discussion on Aryan invasion theory, see Parpola, *The Roots of Hinduism*, 2015; Thapar, "The Theory of Aryan Race and India," 1996.
10 Mill, *The History of British India*, 1817.
11 Sugirtharajah, *Imagining Hinduism*, ix.
12 For a discussion on Hindu–Muslim polarity, see Sharma, "On Hindu, Hindustān, Hinduism and Hindutva," 2002; Thapar, "The Theory of Aryan Race and India," 1996.
13 Jones, "The Four Yugs and Ten Avatars of the Hindoos," 269.
14 Sugirtharajah, *Imagining Hinduism*, 4.
15 For a discussion on the emergence and significance of the word Hindu, see Lorenzen, "Who Invented Hinduism?" 1999; Sharma, "On Hindu, Hindustān, Hinduism and Hindutva," 2002; See also Lochtefeld, *The Illustrated Encyclopedia of Hinduism*, ix.
16 Whaling, *Understanding Hinduism*, 14–15.
17 Brockington, *The Sacred Thread*, 24.
18 Feuerstein et al. offer seventeen arguments on why the Aryan invasion never happened. See Feuerstein et al., *In Search of the Cradle of Civilisation*, 1995.
19 Aurobindo, *The Secret of the Veda*, 553.
20 Thapar, "The Theory of Aryan Race and India," 1996.
21 Ibid., 26.
22 Thapar, "Some Appropriations of the Theory of Aryan Race relating to the Beginnings of Indian History," 19.

23 Jackson, "The Persian Dominions in Northern India Down to the Time of Alexander's Invasion," 324–325.

24 Sharma, "On Hindu, Hindustān, Hinduism and Hindutva," 4.

25 Prabhavananda and Manchester, *The Spiritual Heritage of India*, 7, 22.

26 Ahmad, *Studies in Islamic Culture in the Indian Environment*, 77.

27 Sachau, *Alberuni's India*, 1914.

28 Ibid., 21.

29 Davis, "Introduction," 6–7.

30 Cited in Davis, "Introduction," 6–7.

31 Nag and Burman, *The English Works of Raja Rammohun Roy* (vol. 1), 1.

32 Thapar, *Interpreting Early India*, 79. Ekanath, a popular saint of Maharashtra in the sixteenth century said: "If I call myself a Hindu I will be beaten up, and Muslim I am not." See Joshi and Josh, *Struggle for Hegemony in India 1920-47*, 3.

33 For a discussion on *Bhakti* movement, see Wilson, *The Religious Sects of the Hindus*, 1904; Monier-Williams, *Hinduism*, 1894; Grierson, "Bhakti-Marga," 1910.

34 For a discussion on the role of interpretation in *Bhakti* movement, see Inden, *Imagining India*, 1992; Mishra, *Devotional Poetics and the Indian Sublime*, 1998.

35 Doshi, "Editorial," vii-xii.

36 See Singh, "Manipur Vaishnavism," 66–72.

37 George, *Paths to the Divine*, 226.

38 Shakespear, "The Religion of Manipur," 1913.

39 The Sanskrit text entitled *Dharani Samhita* (1825–1834) has popularized the legends of the derivation of Manipur's name.

40 Sanjeev, "Surveying and Producing the Frontier in Nineteenth Century Manipur," 2019.

41 Arambam, "Preface," 2004.

42 Sanjeev, "Surveying and Producing the Frontier in Nineteenth Century Manipur," 2019.

43 For a discussion on history of Manipur, see Kabui, *History of Manipur*, 1991; Sanajaoba, *Manipur Past and Present*, 2005. Sana, *The Chronology of Meetei Monarchs*, 2010; "National Seminar on "Hinduism in Manipur" on 29–30 June 2018," 2018.

44 For a discussion on *Meitei* religious practices and literature, see Khelchandra, *History of Ancient Manipuri Literature*, 1969; "National Seminar on "Hinduism in Manipur" on 29–30 June 2018," 2018.

45 Singh, *The Unquiet Valley*, 2.

46 See Paratt, *Religion of Manipur*, 136–140.

47 Singh, *The Unquiet Valley*, 3.

48 For a discussion, see Ray, "Boundaries Blurred?" 250, 252.

49 For a discussion, see Bandopadhay, "Dance: The tool of Sanskritisation process in Manipur," 2008.

50 Christianity arrived in Manipur with missionaries and the British officially annexed the princely state with India in the nineteenth century. See Nilabir, "The Revivalist Movement of Sanamahism," 1991.

51 McCulloch, *Account of the Valley of Munnipore and of the Hill Tribes*, 18.

52 Ibid., 17.

53 These kings include Gambhir Singh (1825–1834), Nara Singh (1844–1850), Chandrakirti (1850–1886) and Raja Churachand Singh (1891–1941). See Sana, *The Chronology of Meetei Monarchs*, 2010; "National Seminar on 'Hinduism in Manipur' on 29–30 June 2018," 2018. For a discussion on relationship between mythology and history in Manipur, see Ray, "Boundaries Blurred?" 247–250.

54 Arambam, "Manipur," 57–58.
55 Frykenberg, "The Emergence of Modern 'Hinduism' as a Concept and as an Institution," 31; Also see Lochtefeld, *The Illustrated Encyclopedia of Hinduism*, vii.
56 Smith, *Meaning and End of Religion*, 1963.
57 Sugirtharajah, Imagining Hinduism, 143.
58 Tarabout, "Malabar Gods, Nation-Building and World Culture," 2005.
59 For a discussion on Swami Vivekananda's life and works, See Paranjape and Sengupta, *The Cyclonic Swami*, 2005; Paranjape, *Swami Vivekananda*, 2015.
60 For a discussion on the global appeal of Hinduism, see King, "Orientalism and the Modern Myth of 'Hinduism'," 1999; Lorenzen, "Who Invented Hinduism?" 1999.
61 For a discussion on Gandhian thought, see Paranjape, *Decolonization and Development*, 1993.
62 Gandhi, "Why I Am A Hindu," 1927.
63 Page, *Prelude to Partition*, 73–84.
64 Gould, *Hindu Nationalism and the Language of Politics in Late Colonial India*, 1.
65 The official proposal for a two-state solution to India will come in the 1940s from Muslim League leader Mohammad Ali Jinnah. Savarkar's militant Hinduism and Hindutva ideology in fuelling this solution cannot be neglected.
66 Savarkar, *Hindutva: Who is a Hindu?* 1923/1969.
67 For a discussion on Hindutva and Hinduism, see Anderson and Damle, *The Brotherhood of Saffron*, 1987; Lipner, "On 'Hindutva' and 'Hindu-Catholic', with a Moral for Our Times," 1992; Sharma, "On Hindu, Hindustān, Hinduism and Hindutva," 2002.
68 Savarkar, *Hindutva: Who is a Hindu?* 91.
69 Bakhle, "Country First?" 2010.
70 Banerjee, "'Hindutva': Ideology and Social Psychology," 97; See also Anderson and Damle, *The Brotherhood of Saffron*, 1987.
71 Ibid.
72 Nandy, "The Demonic and the Seductive in Religious Nationalism," 2009.
73 For a detailed discussion on Brahmabandhav Upadhyay, see Lipner, *Life and Thought of a Revolutionary*, 1999.
74 Nandy, "The Demonic and the Seductive in Religious Nationalism," 2.
75 Quoted in Nauriya, "The Savarkarist Syntax," 2014.
76 Nandy, "The Demonic and the Seductive in Religious Nationalism," 2.
77 For a detailed discussion on glorification of Savarkar's ideology, see Basu et al., *Khaki Shorts, Saffron Flags*, 1993; Ghosh, *BJP and the Evolution of Hindu Nationalism*, 2000; Sarkar, *Beyond Nationalist Frames*, 2002; Ram-Prasad, "Contemporary Political Hinduism," 2003.
78 Sharma, *Hindutva*, 2015.
79 In Manipur, as per the 2011 census amongst the three major groups, Hindus comprise 41.39%, Christians 41.29% and Muslims 8.4% of the total population. Despite more than one hundred active RSS *shakhas* (branches) in Manipur, the growth of the BJP in the state has been slow. In the 2017 state election, the BJP with twenty-one seats got the support of four MLAs each from the Naga People's Front and the National Peoples Party and one each from the Lok Janshakti Party and Congress resulting in the first BJP-led government.
80 Nandy, "The Demonic and the Seductive in Religious Nationalism," 3, 6.

81 See Section 6.4 given in "BJP Manipur Pradesh Vision Document 2017," 12.
82 The re-established cultural map for *Akhand Bharat* includes most importantly Afghanistan, Pakistan, India, Tibet, Bangladesh, Nepal, Sri Lanka and Myanmar. For a discussion, see Longkumer, "Playing the Waiting Game," 281–296.
83 For a detailed discussion on Hinduism of the "secular" Congress in the 1930s and 1940s, see Gould, *Hindu Nationalism and the Language of Politics in Late Colonial India*, 2004.
84 Ibid.
85 Ibid., 160. Also, look at the alliances of "secular" Congress with Arya Samaj in late colonial India and there policy of "soft Hindutva" to defeat Narendra Modi-led BJP in 2019.
86 Pathak, "BJP has Insulted My Hinduism," 2019.
87 For a detailed discussion, see Paranjape, *Decolonization and Development*, 1993.
88 Doniger and Nussbaum, *Pluralism and Democracy in India*, 2015.

2 The Hindu Dances of Manipur[1]

Sharada Sugirtharajah writes that Hinduism or the idea of being Hindu "is not confined to texts or to a prescribed set of beliefs."[2] Being Hindu "encompasses a wide variety of other areas such as art, dance, music and folklore."[3] According to Hindu tradition and philosophy, all arts are gifts from God or are ways of accessing Him. The study of Hindu dance or Indian classical dance tells us that this phenomenon has a long history and it still enjoys a popular following far beyond the boundaries of India. In fact, Friedhelm Hardy notes, much exposition on *rasa*, central to theorizations of aesthetics, amalgamates dance, acting, music, specific poetic themes and a particular poetic genre.[4] Many scholars have noted the importance of dance in India, particularly, to Hinduism. For Judith Lynne Hanna, this comes from dance being imbricated with the sacred traditions of religious faith.[5] Dance is passed as and is used to pass on cultural knowledge in many communities. As cultural theorist Stuart Hall puts it, human beings assign meaning through "the frameworks of interpretation which we bring to them."[6] Hindu dance essentially explores the relationship between the primordial human past and the divine. Owing to its association with religion, a Hindu dance space is not just a stage but also a site for the interpretation of the divine force.

In Hinduism, with a number of gods and goddesses, the relationship between dance and religion is intrinsic. *Nritya* (dance) is the reverberation of the five *kriyas* (work) of God—*Avirbhava* (creation), *Isthiti* (preservation), *Samhara* (destruction), *Tirobhava* (illusion) and *Anugraha* (salvation).[7] *Nataraja* (the five-faced Lord Shiva) is the first dancer. In the revival of the Hindu dance tradition, Matthew Harp Allen argues, *Nataraja* became a central metaphor:

> *Nataraja*, an ancient form of the god Siva indigenous to South India, would serve as the perfect *nayaka* (lord) of the revived dance. The astonishingly beautiful bronze sculpture of Nataraja from the Cola

DOI: 10.4324/9781003205203-3

era (ca. 9–11th century C.E.) is today the focus of his renown in the international art world, but even earlier (ca. 530 C.E.), Nataraja was depicted in stone in the Chalukya center of Badami, dancing with the wives of the rishis (sages) in the forest. As we will see, however, despite his deep roots in South Indian religious tradition, Nataraja had never before been asked to play a role quite like the one reserved for him in the twentieth-century revival.[8]

Nataraja performed the vigorous cosmic dance—*tandava*—that resulted in the creation of the earth.[9] His dance form expressed the ecstasy of creation, preservation and destruction. Gregory Bateson observes:

> Consider Shiva, the *Nataraj* figure, the Dancing Shiva. This is a paradigm, imposed upon the entire world of experience, in which it is assumed that everything that happens, ranging from earthquakes to gossip to murder, to joy, to love, to laughter, and all the rest, is an incredible zig-zag of what might seem otherwise to the unclassifiable and discorded experience, but is, in fact, all framed within the Shivaite concept of *The Dance*.[10]

The cosmic dance of Lord Shiva is the manifestation of the rhythms of our lives. The rhythm of the *tandava* and all such other dances were guided by the beat of the drum of Lord Shiva. Gayanacharya Avinash C. Pandeya notes that this life is "the Centre of Universe, i.e., God within the heart."[11]

The traditional Indian dance that developed over the centuries was aided by both Hindu religious and local cultural practices. Hindu temples nurtured dancers and dances told stories from mythology. According to renowned Indian dancer Shovana Narayan, most of these earlier forms of dance were largely solo and hardly any props were used by the dancers. She writes:

> Thus the onus fell on the dancer for effective communication for which they utilised "mudras" (hand gestures), "bhavas," "rasas" (moods of emotions) and expressions for enabling characters and situations to be described. Hence all dance forms were similar in their origin and ultimate aim, as they all originated as the outward manifestation of expression, borne out of deep religious sentiment.[12]

Therefore, a major commonality among all the Hindu dances is the fact that they are deeply rooted in religion. Eminent dance critic and scholar Sunil Kothari adds:

Mythological and devotional stories form their content. The expressive aspect tends to revolve around a *nayika*, the heroine, who pines for union with the *nayaka*, the hero. The heroine symbolises the soul of the devotee, and the hero, the Lord, the super-soul with whom the soul wishes to unite. The spirit of the *bhakti* movement, the cult of devotion, permeates these dance forms.[13]

Under the spirit of *bhakti* (devotion), Hindus saw dance as a means to connect or communicate with the gods.[14] This is one of the reasons that almost all Hindu dances are performed barefoot. Joan Cass in her book *The Dance* observes:

> Hindu dance is the oldest of the world's developed dance forms. Hindu dance depicts a serene and ordered universe. Gracefully intricate hand gestures and subtle facial motions tell a ritualized story from the storehouse of religious legend. There are also Hindu dances that proceed in complex rhythms whose intent is solely the offering of a prescribed pattern of motion for contemplation as a spiritual experience.[15]

The varied Indian classical dance forms, that sprung from diverse traditional Hindu religious, folk or musical theatres of the past, have acquired some key techniques over the years. These include—*mudras* (gestures), *rasas* (aesthetic impression) and *bhava* (mood or emotions)—mentioned in Bharata's *Natyasastra*[16] and Nandikeshwara's *Bharatarnava*. While Bharata mentions eight *rasas*—*Sringara* (Erotic), *Hasya* (Comic), *Karuna* (Pathos), *Raudra* (Furious), *Bhayanaka* (Terrible), *Vira* (Heroic), *Vibhatsa* (Disgust) and *Adbhuta* (Marvellous)—another great Sanskrit commentator Abhinaya Gupta Acharya mentions a ninth *rasa* (*navrasa*)—*Santa* (Tranquil).[17] Three classes of *bhavas* are produced with an interplay of emotions: *Sattvika* (physical), *Manasika* (action of the mind) and *Saririka* (bodily action). *Natyasastra* (the science of dance) encompasses elements of dance, drama, dialogue and music that attempts also to highlight the core "Indianness" of many varied dance forms.[18] The four kinds of actions (*abhinayas*)—Sattvika (emotional attributes), *Angika* (body gestures), *Vacka* (vocal) and *Aharya* (dress)—are attached importance.[19] In relation to dance, the treatise mentions postures and gaits—10 *mandalas* (modes of standing), 6 *sthankas* (modes of resting), 5 *utplavanas* (kinds of leaps), 7 *bhramaris* (kinds of pirouettes), 32 *caris* (gaits), 28 *asamyukta hastas* (single hand gestures), 24 *samyukta hastas* (combined hand gestures) and 30 *nritta hastas* (ornate gestures).[20] The techniques mentioned in ancient Indian treatises on the performing arts have been incorporated into all the Indian classical dance forms.[21]

With constant invasions, especially Muslim (Mughal) and Christian (British), and an international platform, the original dance techniques were constantly modulated to create new forms. Rita Vega de Triana observes that the wandering dancing gipsies too made innovations in dance styles possible: "It is recorded that Hindu dancers performed in the summer palace at Cadiz for the royal Spanish court, and their highly formalized gesture language must have extended some influence on what became the 'Andalucian style.'"[22] In fact, the modulation and mixing are, to an extent, responsible for similarities between Spanish Flamenco and some Hindu dances. She writes:

> As in Flamenco, the Hindu dance makes use of the hand-clap (the Spanish "palma," the Hindu "tala"). It is an essential element in timing and rhythm. The Hindi "Jhaptal" is similar to the flamenco "Bulerias" in that the hand-claps are arranged in a two-three-two-three pattern. The Indian "Chautal" is marked in steady beats of twelve, as is the flamenco "Soleares" and the "Alegrias."[23]

With time, Hindu religiosity was replaced by spirituality. But the basic rhythm, theme and expression remain the same.[24] Sitara Thobani notes that in most of the Indian classical dances:

> ... the spiritual offers an abstract, almost universal relevance for the dance that is not dependent (at first glance) on its Hindu identification. With the origins of Indian classical dance in Hinduism already taken for granted, dancers quickly identify spirituality as the medium for their contemporary experiences in dance.[25]

Kothari observes that in addition to temples, where the dance was a part of the ritual procedures, the royal courts of India offered patronage to dancers, and to their art.[26]

Institutions figuring women dancers were common—*devadasis, nagar badhus, bhagtans, kalavangtis or Maibi.*[27] *Devadasis* (female servant of God), popular in South India, were symbolically married to God and on auspicious occasions performed temple rituals or festivities.[28] In Hinduism, the residing deity of the temple is treated like an earthly king.[29] The God has a court just like the local king would, with ministers, musicians and dancers. Soon, this became a hereditary practice and the children of these *devadasis* continued the same profession and also performed the role of courtesans, mistresses, musicians and temple workers.[30]

During British rule, Hindu dance forms, especially temple dancing, were looked down upon and the women performers—*devadasis*—were increasingly treated like prostitutes. Amrit Srinivasan in "Reform and Revival" outlines the events that led to the banning of the *devadasi* system, particularly of dedicating young girls to temples.[31] During the late nineteenth and early twentieth centuries, the total elimination of the *devadasi* system was demanded by reformers in the form of anti-*nautch* campaigns.[32] The critics of temple dancing, reformists and national leaders focussed on *devadasis* and *nautch* girls' sexual lives and presented them as victims of colonial society.

During the course of these debates, and partly in reaction to the policies of the colonial government, a revival movement started in India with the aim of creating a national identity through indigenous arts. To facilitate this transformation, or rescue temple dance and embody it with spiritual meaning devoid of secular sensuality, it was necessary for would-be reformers to exclude *devadasis'* from the discourse of the re-creation of classical dance. This reform movement, led mostly by middle-class and upper-caste men and women, saw a pressing need for the development of the arts and patronized "purified." Hindu dance and devotional music. Cultural revivalists and Hindu activists believed that this pure or ideal art must draw on asexualized Hindu idioms and be performed by ideal women.

Also, as part of a larger pattern of revival and promotion, intellectuals and artists from North, South and East India such as Gurudev Rabindranath Tagore (in Bengal), Vallathol (in Kerala), Rukmini Devi (in Chennai), Madame Menaka (in Mumbai) and Uday Shankar (in Almora) founded institutions for training in Indian dance, music and the arts through the 1930s.[33] Their attempts were supported by frequent visits of Western dancers such as Ragini, La Marie, Anna Pavlova and many others. These dancers asked young, educated Indians to learn and promote the arts.[34] In fact, two Prime Ministers of India—Pundit Jawaharlal Nehru and his daughter Indira Gandhi—had a special affection for the Manipuri dance form. Indira Gandhi (PM 1967–1977 and again, 1980–1984), learned Manipuri dance at Santiniketan as a young girl. Her love of the form abided, and she invariably included Manipuri dancers as part of her cultural delegation on visits to foreign countries.

Hindu dance and music was seen simultaneously as classical and national, and such as foregrounded Hindu religious beliefs.[35] Kothari points out that at most upcoming local dance centres and institutions, learning classical Indian dance was pursued by young women from the educated middle class. As pioneering women from upper-class Brahmin backgrounds such as Rukmini Devi Arundale[36] took up the *devadasi* form of *sadhir*, "the stigma attached to dance was not completely removed, but the change in attitude was noticeable."[37]

According to Amrit Srinivasan, the revival movement was created mostly by the Brahmin leaders and hardly acknowledged the *devadasis*. For the arts, the traditional form of patronage had been funded from princely states and wealthy patrons. In his book Traditions of Indian Classical Dance,[38] dance critics and collectors of heritage items Mohan Khokar observes that, gradually, Indian classical dance moved away from its original form—from being controlled by temples to becoming a commercial market enterprise.[39]

Classical Indian dance and institutions promoting it were firmly established when India gained independence in 1947. Present representations of Indian classical dance are extensions of the nationalist and post-colonial discourse.[40] The tradition of royal patronage was replaced by funding from government organizations. In national and state development plans, Indian governments began sponsoring bodies to promote the local arts, especially classical art forms and literature. Sanasam Gourahari Singh, an ex-officio Secretary of the Jawaharlal Nehru Manipuri Dance Academy (JNMDA), writes that it was Nehru who insisted that Manipuri dance, and the philosophies that propagated and fuelled it, were "worth preserving and spreading."[41] He further adds that Nehru was clear about maintaining its historical locality.

> The idea of establishing a college of Manipuri dance strongly worked in his mind and he started taking steps in order that there might not be any missing link in the stream. He rejected the proposal of some of his advisors connected with cultural affairs to locate it somewhere in Shillong or other places outside Manipur. To ensure the unfailing growth of the pristine purity of Manipuri dancing his argument was that its study should be conducted within its native environments, Manipur.[42]

Established in the 1950s, the Sangeet Natak Akademi (1953), the Jawaharlal Nehru Manipur Dance Academy (1954) and the Sahitya Natak Akademi (1954) aim to foster and promote India's music, drama and literature.[43]

Various styles of Indian classical dance, including Bharatanatyam, Kathakali, Mohiniyattam, Manipuri and Odissi, have long been associated with Hinduism.[44] Sitara Thobani argues that these dance performances were based on the modern interpretation and understanding

of Hindu practice—"especially in the context of the nationalist movement that saw (and continues to see) the convergence of Hindu identity
with Indian nationality."[45] During the nationalist phase, however, the
revival of Hindu dance with an unbroken ancient tradition also came to
be associated with the construction of India's secular national identity.
The concept of a common heritage of all dances provided an umbrella
under the term Indian classical dance, where various styles were meant
to be fostered together.[46] The Government of India's Ministry of
Culture reorganized eleven key dance forms in a composite category
called *Bhartiya shastriya nritya* (Indian classical dance)—Bharatanatyam,
Kathakali, Kuchipudi, Manipuri, Kathak, Mohiniyattam, Odissi,
Sattriya, Chhau, Gaudiya Nritya and Thang Ta—while the *Sangeet
Natak Akademi* (The National Academy for Music, Dance and Drama)
recognizes only eight of these forms.[47] But even today, the characterization and coding of most of these Indian classical dances as manifestations of a Hindu religious tradition are maintained for both national
and international audiences. This is done, first, through the use of gods
and goddesses such as Shiva, Durga, Rama, Sita, Radha and Krishna that
dominate dance performance and inscribe the performance within the
spiritual space of the temple through invocations. Second, it is facilitated
through the placement of the *Nataraja* statue on stage. As discussed at the
beginning of this chapter, Lord Shiva is seen as the central icon of Hindu
dance.

In this context, Sitara Thobani argues that by placing Lord Shiva, the
deity of dance, on the stage, audiences are reminded of the religious,
Hindu origins of Indian classical dance. She writes:

> Placing these deities on stage conveys to the audience the primacy of
> the divine over the performance, as well as to recall the supposedly
> longstanding history that ties together temple dance with contem-
> porary classical dance … they also further assumptions of the dance
> as unequivocally Hindu in the most static of terms… the apparently
> Hindu characterization of the dance is maintained for audiences
> who are taught that the religious attributes of Indian classical dance
> are woven into its secular performance.[48]

The key figure in promoting *Nataraja* as the symbol of the grandeur of
Hindu dance and religion was historian and philosopher A. K.
Coomaraswamy. His 1918 essay "The Dance of Shiva" has arguably
been the most influential publication in the remarkable popularization of
Nataraja as a patron deity and new subject for the aesthetic significance of

revived dance out of India.[49] The dance of *Nataraja* represents the cosmic activity of Lord Shiva. He writes:

> The movement of the dancing figure is so admirably balanced that while it fills all space, it seems nevertheless to be at rest, in the sense that a spinning top or a gyrostat is at rest; thus realising the unity and simultaneity of the five activities (*Pancakrtya*, vise., Production, Maintenance, Destruction, Embodiment and Release) which the symbolism specifically designates.[50]

Coomaraswamy sees *Nataraja's* dance as an interplay of the feminine *Prakriti* (nature) and the masculine *Purusha* (omnipresent spirit). He summarizes his argument regarding the essential significance of the dance of Shiva thus:

> First, it is the image of his Rhythmic Play as the Source of all Movement within the Cosmos, which is Represented by the Arch: Secondly, the Purpose of his Dance is to Release the Countless souls of men from the Snare of Illusion: Thirdly the Place of the Dance, Chidambaram, the Centre of the Universe, is within the Heart.[51]

So, with the origins of Indian classical dance in Hinduism already taken for granted by the audiences, maintenance of the religious specificity of the performance itself is imposed through *Nataraja*.[52] Though Rukmini Devi was one of the first Indian dancers of renown to place Natraja and to create the temple atmosphere on stage as a precursor to performance, there is no scholarly agreement on how and when, precisely, the practice began.[53]

Compared to other classical Indian dances, most Manipuri dances are less descriptive, and less overtly symbolic a manifestation of deeply ritualistic tradition.[54] According to Bimbavati Devi, exponent of Manipuri dance and daughter of renowned dancers Kalavati Devi and the Late Guru Bipin Singh, all Indian dance styles have their special characteristics.[55]

> Manipuri is very free flowing and the movements are lyrical like waves. One of the unique features of this dance form is that the *lasya* and *tandava* aspects are different from each other. Even the costumes are different. *Lasya* is soft and has subtle movements, while *tandava* is vigorous. The torso movement of our dance form is yet another unique feature.[56]

In Manipur, the dance revolved around *Maibi (or Maibee)*—the priestesses and ritual guardians of the Umang Lai, an indigenous faith associated with the spiritual life of the *Meitei* and Chakpa people (Figure 2.1).[57] It is generally believed that through their dance skills and harnessing of spiritual energy, *Maibis* communicate directly with the deities and supernatural forces.[58] Unlike the *devadasi* system of South India, Manipur's *Maibi* could lead a normal married life and work at the local temple.[59] Celebrated Indian choreographer Kumudini Lakhia notes that in Manipur, the tradition of dance has been very pervasive and dance is a part of daily life, rituals and festivals held around the year.[60] This is reflected in Manipur's most popular dances which are:

- *Maibi Jagoi*: a pre-Hindu ritualistic priestess dance;
- *Thang Ta*: an ancient martial art form;
- *Lai Haraoba (or Lai Haraoba)*: literally meaning the merry-making of

Figure 2.1 Ima Santi Amaibi in the Maibi's trance dance—the *Kanglei Thokpa*, known also as *Lai Nupi Thiba* (The Lai searching for their bride) from *Koubru Lai Haraoba*, Thangmeiband, West Imphal, 2015.

Source: Photographer: Byron Aihara.

Photograph Courtesy: With one-time use permission of the photographer and filmmaker Byron Aihara, Seven Sisters Music, USA.

gods and goddesses, is a traditional festival dance celebrating deities and ancestors;

- *Ras Lila (or Ras Leela)*: a Vaishnavite dance drama about Radha and Krishna's love;
- *Pung Cholom*: a drum dance usually performed as a prelude to the *Ras Lila*;
- *Khamba-Thoibi*: a dance performed as part of *Lai Haraoba*;
- *Lasya*: a dance performed by Goddess Parvathi expressing happiness and beauty; and
- *Sankirtan (or Natasankirtan)*: a complex dance and song performance with strict codes involving a group of male drum and cymbal dancers praising the qualities in Radha and Lord Krishna.[61]

Baldeo Sahai writes that the theme of Manipuri dances is various moods of nature or the episodes of Lord Krishna. So, the ideal for a Manipuri dancer is to recreate the grace, innocence and *rasas* from the life of Lord Krishna.[62] According to Guru Bipin Singh, Manipuri dance strictly observes the codification evolved by the Vaishnava text *Ujjvalanilamani* written by Shri Rupa Goswami.[63] All elements of the Manipuri dance, in both dance-dramas and individual performances, composition, choreography, costumes, music and rhythm patterns are determined by specific rules and regulations. The final balance in dance movements is achieved by avoiding emphasis on any one part of the body.

Three Manipuri dance forms are of particular interest to the journey of Hindu dance in Australia. These dances are also the most popular performance styles of Manipur. The first is *Khamba*, it also goes by the Assamese name *Jagoi*, a form of *nritya* (dance) which is a purely rhythmical and dramatic dance performed with drums and cymbals.[64] It tells the tragic love story of an orphan boy Khamba and princess Thoibi from the epic *Moirang Parba*.[65] The central theme of the story, according to Sruti Bandopadhay, is "freedom of women's love."[66] Khamba is based on extra-marital love, its acceptance and ultimately a "divine realization of human consciousness."[67]

The second dance style which has borrowed heavily from *Khamba* is *Lai Haraoba*. It is a form based on a unique creation story that deals particularly with human beings' relationship to the earth, nature, and work patterns, as opposed to the now popular Hindu mythical version.[68] According to Kothari:

> The pre-Vaishnavite tradition of *Lai Haraoba*, the merry-making of the gods and a vibrant tradition of *Thang-ta*, a martial art wielding sword and spear and practiced by both men and women, offer a

dancer a staggering variety of movements to draw upon. Nowhere in India is dance and music so interwoven with rituals and religious practice. One rarely comes across any Manipuri who does not know dance and music.[69]

The *Maibas* and *Maibis* (male priest and female priestess) play a major role in the *Lai Haraoba* performance. According to E. Nilkanta Singh, the *Lai Haraoba* dance involves a sequence of complicated rituals.[70] These are:

* *Lai Ekauba* and *Lai Themba* (to summon the gods);
* *Laikaba* (arrival of the gods and goddesses);
* *Lai Hunba* (throwing of flowers);
* *Jibanyas* (infusion of life);
* *Jagoi Okpa* (reception to the gods);
* *Lai Chingba* (elaborate dance movements of the Maibis);
* *Lai Pou* (birth of god);
* building of a house by the Maibis; and
* dance of the different stages of fishing by the Maibis.[71]

There are three kinds of traditions of *Lai Haraoba*—*Chakpa*, the *Konglei* and the *Moirang*.[72] Both *Jagoi* and *Lai Haraoba* involve delicate shaping of the body, subtle movements and precise choreography; they often take the audiences directly to mystical realms of *Gandharvas*.[73] American linguist and critic Faubion Bowers note that Manipur was famous as a sub-nation of dancers and musicians.[74] In the ancient Hindu epics such as *Ramayana* and *Mahabharata*, Manipur, also known as Sanaaleibaak, Meitrabaak or Kangleipaak,[75] was presented as the home of these ce- lestial dancers. In epics, Manipur has its origins in a mythical tale where the great snake god emerged from the centre of the earth and in ecstasy, sprayed diamonds. In mythological tales of the *Mahabharata* and *Vedas*, Princess Usha, daughter of King Banasur of Multan, who married Krishna's grandson Prince Anirudha, was an expert *Lasya* dancer trained by Goddess Parvati herself. Well-known Manipuri dancer and academic Sohini Ray calls it a "highly charged political text" and has shown how this religious folklore has been utilized over the years to promote "no- tions of racial identity among the *Meitei* people of north-eastern India."[76]

The third dance form is *Ras Lila* which denotes the phenomenal cosmic dance of Krishna, Radha and the *gopis* (milkmaids). The first production of *Ras Lila* dates back to 1779 and was initiated by King Bhagyachandra. But, it was Guru Amubi Singh (also known as Oja Amubi) who developed and made it famous. *Ras Lila* includes the following types: *maha raas, basanta raas, nitya raas, kunja raas* and *diva raas* (Figure 2.2). *Ras Lila* in the traditional sense comprises a circle dance in which several feminine figures (*gopis*) surround a masculine one (Krishna) who occupies centre-stage. The deities Krishna and Radha are brought out of their rooms in the temple, placed on the centre of the mandala and the dancers go around the deities singing and dancing.[77] It depicts Krishna's loveplay and the *gopis'* devotion through performance. In *Ras Lila*, the dancers keep their faces covered with a thin veil. Sruti Bandopadhay explains that this practice is "to divert the attention of the onlookers from the face of the artist."[78] Saryu Doshi observes that as the dancers move around Lord Krishna and Radha in grandeur, the "devotional fervour… lifts the participants and the audience into an exalted state of consciousness."[79] These performances are considered an integral part of the ritualistic practices of the Lord Krishna devotees in Vaishnavism.[80] In support of this argument, Angana Jhaveri notes that in a *Ras Lila* performance "religion and rituals play a significant role."[81] She explains that in essence the theme of *Ras Lila* is romantic (Figure 2.3). It

Figure 2.2 A moment from *Maha Ras Lila* at Shree Shree Gonvidaji temple, located on the royal palace grounds, Imphal, 2017.

Source: Photographer: Byron Aihara.

Photograph Courtesy: With one-time use permission of the photographer and filmmaker Byron Aihara, Seven Sisters Music, USA.

Figure 2.3 Iche Chandan Devi as Radha and Thoibi as Krishna in the Jawaharlal
Nehru Manipur Dance Academy stage production of *Basanta Ras Lila*,
Imphal, 2014.

Source: Photographer: Byron Aihara.

Photograph Courtesy: With one-time use permission of the photographer and filmmaker
Byron Aihara, Seven Sisters Music, USA.

"exemplifies the sublime *vaishnava* view that the arts have the capacity to
express the divine."[82] She further adds that the "performances of the
raslila are considered to be auspicious and are revered by the Krishna-
bhaktas (devotees) of Manipur, whose utmost concern is to safeguard the
tradition."[83]

Renowned Indian writer and critic Mulk Raj Anand, in his editorial
piece for a special issue of journal *Marg,* highlighted how Manipuri

dance has remained on the borders of the Indian classical and the folk.
He points out:

> ... in spite of the high order of the classical Manipuri style, its
> subtleties and intricacies of co-ordination of the hand gestures, the
> foot-work and the *abhinaya* (facial expressions), we always get the
> echoes of ecstatic people. The borderline between the classical and
> the folk, therefore, remains uncannily near. And rather than detract
> from the beauty or grace of the finished Manipuri style, the echoes
> of vital folk movements impart to this style a peculiar intimacy.[84]

The folk elements have remained dominant in Manipuri dance for much
longer than in other Indian dances.[85] Two reasons for the dominance of
the folk elements are: (a) the availability of limited resources and (b)
dance was never removed from the festivity or ritualistic practices to
become bare individual performance.[86] Sruti Bandopadhay notes that in
Manipur the dance is still presented as a temple performance along with
its elaborate rituals. She explains:

> The reason behind the continuity till date of this tradition is the
> participation of the community. The dance was never extracted
> from social festivities or ritualistic practices to be performed by
> individuals. The duty of the principal dancer is to lead a group of
> dancers to the place of performance and guide their involvement in
> the ritual.... The ceremony of rituals is always around the deity and
> on the public premises of the temple.[87]

The *Meitei* community participates in the various dance performances
held throughout the year.[88] With reference to *Ras Lila* receiving little
attention, Angana Jhaveri observes:

> The performers include professionals and non-professionals enabling
> community members who may have had only some training to
> participate. Children play a major role, as only they may play the
> deified roles of Krishna and Radha. The royal family takes an
> especially active interest as the tradition is as much of the court as it
> is of the temple. Learned *gurus* (masters), the elders and those of the
> *brahmanic* orders are given an elevated position in the event, and
> attend most enthusiastically. And so, at any *raslila* performance,
> almost every facet of the Manipuri community is represented.[89]

In her article, "In Search of a Secular in Contemporary Indian Dance," Ananya Chatterjea observes:

> Manipuri is a form that has received fewer resources and much less attention than the other classical forms and, despite the later reformulation of the aesthetic via Vaishnavism, still is different from other forms.[90]

In the early 1950s, Manipuri dance and literature were both grappling with the loss of patronage and funds and their paucity became a cause for grave concern, as there were not many sponsors or publishers in Manipur for creative and scholarly works. The artistes and authors had to depend on small subsidies of private patrons or the Government of India for the dissemination of their works.[91] The major reasons for this lack of resources and support were chiefly Manipur's history, geographic location and culture—a history that dates back to 33 AD, a geography of rugged hills and narrow valleys, and a secular culture primarily dominated by an ethnic group called *Meiteis*.[92]

It is said that the seven major clans Khábá, Cenglei, Luwáng, Khuman, Moiráng, Angom and Ningthoujá integrated to form the *Meiteis*.[93] Now Manipur has five social groups all prefixed with the traditional term *Meitei*—the *Meitei marup* (who follow traditional *Meitei* culture and God), *Meitei* Christians, *Meitei goura Chaytonya* (who follow *Meitei* and Hindu gods), the *Meitei Brahmins* (Manipuri Brahmins) and the *Meitei* Muslims (also known as *Miah Meitei* or *Pangal*). When the British were trying to conquer Assam and Manipur, they met a string resistances from the tribal groups. *Meiteis* knew that outsiders, especially the Christian missionaries, despised their "pagan art" and dance forms and a change of ruler would result in the slow death of their culture.

According to M. Sajjad Hassan, pre-colonial Manipur was principally "a centralised state in the centre of the Valley region and village-based autonomous authorities in the surrounding Hills."[94] This "institutional duality" was enforced by the British post-1891 Anglo-Manipur war.[95] In 1949, India merged Manipur using both political and military strategies. According to John Parratt, the tension and conflict between post-colonial India and Manipur increased when the first Prime Minister of India Jawaharlal Nehru visited the newly annexed state and refused to grant it full statehood.[96] Characterizing the situation as "sensitive," in 1958, the Government of India enforced the Armed Forces Special Powers Act (AFSPA). From 1962 until 1972, it was a Union Territory, ruled directly by the Government of India.

Like other north-eastern states of India, which have been trying to establish their independent identities, Manipur too has a grotesque and brutal history of bloodshed and anti-mainland feeling.[97] Ever since its inception, it has seen both small and large-scale, multi-lateral ethnic violence, insurgency and state repression. In the 1950s, the *Kukis* and *Nagas,* who had settled in the hill areas of Manipur, were demanding a separate state, which quickly set the entire region competing for demands of statehood based on tribal affiliations.[98] These demands were seen as a political hindrance to the separatist and nationalist movement of the United National Liberation Front (UNLF) dedicated to Manipuri secession.

The 1950s was also a phase when Manipuri people were struggling to search for their culture and its roots. According to Guru Rao Bapat, an eminent scholar of Indian classical dance: "These efforts that began in pre-independent India, can be seen as part of the effort of projecting a national tradition in opposition to the colonial discourse."[99] There was a "bold assertion" of a distinctive style of life with their rich old literature, folklore, an independent script allied to *Brahmi* and dance forms.[100] This was primarily undertaken under the patronage of King Churachand Maharaj (1891–1941), who contributed substantially to the expansion of the cultural resources of Manipur, especially in the fields of performance and sports. In 1922, the king sent a 150-member troupe, under Guru Amubi and Guru Atomba, to Calcutta (now Kolkata) to present *Ras Lila* to the visiting Prince Albert. But what ultimately became known as Manipuri dance was a simplification and interpretation of the authentic dance forms of *Maibi* and *Khamba* by the noted Bengali poet and Noble Laureate Gurudev Rabindranath Tagore in 1919.[101]

While the Uday Shankar India Cultural Centre was established in 1928 and Kalakshetra was established by Rukmini Devi in 1936, Indian dance was made a part of the core syllabus at Tagore's Visva-Bharati as early as in 1925. According to Santidev Ghosh, Tagore pioneered this movement for the revival of Indian classical dance with the help of well-known dance teachers and students of Santiniketan and Visva-Bharati (founded 1921).[102] Here, the key features of the syllabus were—classes in Manipuri dances, south Indian Tala dances, training in Bol and symbolic Mundra, Kathakali dance, rendering of Bengali songs to dances and dramatic interpretation. For Tagore, Utpal K. Banerjee observes, the dominant dance form of Manipuri was an extension or an expression of poetry or emotions through the body's rhythm.[103]

Today, there are many *Rabindra Sangit* (music) and *Rabindra Nritiya Natya* (dance drama), like *Chitrangada,* which involves Manipuri dances.[104] According to Saryu Doshi, Manipuri dance entered the Indian urban cultural landscape when Gurudev Tagore and Uday Shankar started inviting

Manipuri dance artistes and gurus (such as Amobi Singh) to teach and assist them with the choreography of several of their dance-dramas at Santiniketan and Almora. According to Smriti Kumar Sinha, apart from the aesthetic and spiritual appeal of Manipur's dances, Tagore used this form as a bridge to help him create a Bengali cultural identity. She notes that Tamil Nadu, Kerala and Orissa had fully developed state dance forms such as Bharatanatyam, Kathakali and Odissi. But Bengal which was "the epicentre of Indian literary, cultural and political revolution, had no dance form of its own of that stature."[105] To fill this gap, Tagore created a "fusion of aesthetically rich Manipuri dance elements and poetically rich Rabindra Sangeet" to give birth to a new dance form—Rabindra Nrityanatya.[106]

Ghosh adds that between 1926 and 1929, at Santiniketan, a number of Manipuri teachers gave expression to Tagore's musical compositions through Manipuri dance styles. It was from here that Manipuri dance spread to the rest of India. Some of these dancers included Budhimantra Singh, Naba Kumar, Senarik Singh Rajkumar, Nileshwar Mukherji, Bihari Singha, Nabakumar Singha, Muhu Singha, Atomba Singh and Amubi Singh.[107] Some well-known exponents of Manipuri dance carried the movement and Tagore's project of popularizing the dance among the "urban intelligentsia" of the country.[108] But Tagore's death (in 1941), Ghosh remembers, marked the end of the formative period of the Manipuri dance movement at Santiniketan.[109] In later years, Guru Amubi Singh (at JNMDA) and Guru Bipin Singh (at Manipuri Nartanalaya) changed the institution of Manipuri dance by creating institutes.[110] Their collaboration with students and other artists was an important step in making Manipuri dance visible to audiences, in academic research and in innovation towards solo performance.[111] These Gurus and their academies played a significant role in moving the sacred Manipuri dance from temples to the stage.[112] Ironically, all the recognition and awards that Manipuri artistes such as Guru Bipin Singh and others received also aggravated debates within Manipur over the implications of how Manipuri dance arrived at its status: "How is it possible to create a Manipuri culture away from Manipuri culture, dependent only on the approval of non-Manipuris?"[113]

The above imperative question had a very close connection with the relation between India and Manipur. As Manipuri dance is an amalgamation of various other forms, its growth under the rubric of "Indian Classical Dance" was also seen as a political stance of the Indian state at integrating Manipur and assimilating Manipuri dance into the dominant culture of India. It was thus interlinked with the development of both Indian and Manipuri nationalism, the constitution of the Indian nation-state and the post-colonial negotiations of Manipur with other Indian states.[114] Partha Chatterjee, in his book *Nationalist Thought and Colonial*

World, has illustrated how the complex relationship between nationalist discourse and colonial domination in the formation of the Indian nation-state itself worked in India's prototypically Third World struggle for self-determination and national integration.[115] During the nationalist phase in the early twentieth century, the revival of Indian classical dances like Bharatanatyam came to be intimately associated with the construction of India's national identity. Other prominent dances, such as Manipuri, Mohiniattam and Kathakali, were re-worked as variations of the system that created Bharatanatyam, so that they could also share in its national and international recognition. M. N. Srinivas notes that the Sanskritisation of groups external to Hinduism, such as tribal people, drew them "into the Hindu fold" which, in addition to the adoption of customs, rituals, beliefs, ideology and style of life of the dominant group, meant the creation of local, hierarchical castes.[116] According to Phanjoubam, as there was no inclusive Manipuri identity, until then was almost synonymous with the *Meitei*, the *Vaishnavite* culture presented an "easier" idiom for the rest of India to identify with and speak of in terms of unification.[117] Nevertheless, Sruti Bandopadhay, a distinguished Manipur dancer herself, believes that "while adopting the Hindu frame of living, as an effect of Sanskritisation, the Meiteis never dissociated from their innate indigenous sensibilities."[118] Adding to this view, Usham Rojio observes that the greater elements of *Meitei* identity, worldview, social resilience and performative traditions have existed as a unified meta-narrative while borrowing and merging ideas from Sanskrit tradition.[119]

Against this historical and socio-political background, it is clear that the performing arts, cultural productions and aesthetic traditions of Manipur were and have remained vulnerable.[120] It was amongst such turmoil that Rajkumar Priyogopal Singh and Ibetombi Devi thought of taking Manipuri dances out of India onto a global stage. They had heard or seen the success of great Uday Shankar, Ram Gopal and Ananda Shivaram.[121] Recognizing the importance of marketing and collaboration with a western impresario, they agreed to create experimental hybridization of their productions to the extent where a positive cross-cultural exchange could take place without undermining their own talent or profaning the nature of Hindu dance.

Notes

1 Parts of this chapter have appeared as "The Hindu dance" in *The Dancing God: Staging Hindu Dance in Australia* (2020). Published here with the permission of Routledge.
2 Sugirtharajah, *Imagining Hinduism*, 140.

3 Ibid.
4 Hardy, *Viraha Bhakti*, 600.
5 Hanna, *Dance, Sex and Gender*, 97.
6 Hall, *Representation*, 3.
7 Pandeya, *The Art of Kathakali*, 1.
8 Allen, "Rewriting the Script for South Indian Dance," 64.
9 For a discussion of various forms of *taṇḍava*, see Chandra, *Encyclopaedia of Hindu Gods and Goddesses*, 121; Coomaraswamy, *The Dance of Shiva*, 1975.
10 Bateson, "Play and Paradigm," 14.
11 Pandeya, *The Art of Kathakali*, xi.
12 Narayan, *The Sterling Book of Indian Classical Dances*, 10.
13 Kothari, "New Directions in Indian Dance," 2008.
14 Narayan, *The Sterling Book of Indian Classical Dances*, 9.
15 Cass, *The Dance*, 28.
16 Often referred to as the fifth *veda* in Hinduism.
17 Pandeya, *The Art of Kathakali*, 95.
18 Shah, "State Patronage in India," 138.
19 Ibid., 4.
20 Narayan, *The Sterling Book of Indian Classical Dances*, 12.
21 Bharata's *Natyasastra*, written between 200 BCE and 200 CE, is considered the fifth *veda* (Sanskrit scripture). Containing 6000 *slokas/sutras* (verse stanzas) on the theory of *bhavas* and *rasas* used in classical performing arts (theatre, dance, and music), it has had a key influence on classical playwrights and dancers. According to this treatise, the god Brahma, Creator of the World, invented the art and science of classical dance and then taught it to the most reverend sage Bharata, who passed on this art to divine beings and humans to enlighten them. Other Indian art dance forms yet to be recognized as classical dance are *Andhra Natyam*, *Vilasini Nrityam/Natyam*, and *Kerala Natanam*.
22 De Triana, *Antonio Triana and the Spanish Dance*, 94.
23 Ibid.
24 Ibid.
25 Thobani, *Indian Classical Dance and the Making of Postcolonial National Identities*, 2017.
26 Kothari, "New Directions in Indian Dance: An Overview 1980–2006," 2008.
27 Narayan, *The Sterling Book of Indian Classical Dances*, 17.
28 For a comprehensive historical portrait of devadasis and the social reform in South India, see Soneji, *Unfinished Gestures*, 2012.
29 Kersenboom-Story, *Nityasumangali*, 1987.
30 Soneji, *Unfinished Gestures*, 3.
31 Srinivasan, "Reform and Revival," 1985; See also Kersenboom-Story, *Nityasumangali*, 1987; Chakravorty, *Bells of Change*, 2008.
32 Anandhi, "Representing Devadasis," 746.
33 Kothari, "New Directions in Indian Dance," 2008; Purkayastha, "Dancing Otherness," 2012.
34 Pandeya, *The Art of Kathakali*, xii.
35 Bakhle, *Two Men and Music*, 2005.
36 Kothari, *Bharata Natyam*, 166–167.
37 Kothari, "New Directions in Indian Dance," 2008.
38 Khokar, Traditions of Indian Classical Dance, 1979.
39 Purie, "Dance Forms," 1979.

40 See also Chakravorty, "From Interculturalism to Historicism," 108.

41 Singh, "Extract from 1970 Annual Function Report," 1970.

42 Ibid.

43 Katrak, *Contemporary Indian Dance*, 36. For further discussion, see Sebastian, "Cultural Fusion in a Religious Dance Drama," 320–321.

44 Meduri, "Labels, Histories, Politics," 2008a; Allen, "Rewriting the Script for South Indian Dance," 1997; Kothari *Bharata Natyam*, 2007.

45 Thobani, *Indian Classical Dance and the Making of Postcolonial National Identities*, 147.

46 Chakravorty, "From Interculturalism to Historicism," 111.

47 For a discussion of the development of Indian dance forms, see Bose, "The Evolution of Classical Indian Dance Literature," 1989; Shah, "State Patronage in India," 2002.

48 Thobani, *Indian Classical Dance and the Making of Postcolonial National Identities*, 153.

49 Coomaraswamy, *The Dance of Shiva*, 1975.

50 Coomaraswamy, *History of Indian and Indonesian Art*, 127.

51 Coomaraswamy, *The Dance of Shiva*, 77.

52 Thobani, *Indian Classical Dance and the Making of Postcolonial National Identities*, 157.

53 See Allen, "Rewriting the Script for South Indian Dance," 79; Ramnarayan, "Rukmini Devi: Dancer and Reformer, a Profile," 29.

54 Vatsyayan, "Introduction," xii–xx.

55 Guru Bipin Singh was a disciple of the late Guru Amudon Sharma, a direct descendant of the gurus to the royal family of Manipur. His father Laikhomsana Singh was a *maiba* and mother Indubala Devi was a well-known singer. Guru Bipin Singh's school, Manipuri Nartanalaya (founded in 1972), follows the tradition of the royal temple in the core traditional choreographies. In August 2014, Sanjib Bhattacharya and Jagannath Lairenjam organized 'Guru Bipin Singh Association India and Abroad' in New York to honour the memory of their legendary guru who during his lifetime despite several invitations never travelled to North America. The Guru Bipin Singh Memorial Award was presented to Nabaghana Shaym Singha, Christel Stevens, Shantibala Sinha and Sohini Ray who have dedicated their lives to popularizing Manipuri Dance in the west. In August 2018, Sohini Ray under the auspices of her dance institution Manipuri Dance Visions organized Guru Bipin Singh's birth centenary in Barnard College, Columbia University, where three generations of Guru Bipin Singh's students performed.

56 Mathew, "A tête-à-tête with Bimbavati Devi, Manipuri Dance Exponent," 2004.

57 For a detailed discussion on role of *maibis*, see Brara, *Politics, Society and Cosmology in India's North East*, 136. According to documentary filmmaker Byron Aihara, around 150–180 *maibis* are still present in Manipur. See Aihara, "A Lesson with the *Maibi* of Manipur: Ima Dhoni Amaibi," 2016.

58 Ibid.

59 Narayan, *The Sterling Book of Indian Classical Dances*, 54. Also see, Chaki-Sircar, *Feminism in a Traditional Society*, 213–214.

60 Lakhia, "Innovations in Kathak," 2003.

61 For a brief discussion on *Khutthek* (the hand gestural movement) used in various Manipuri dances, see Biswas, "Hasta in Manipuri," 2020.

62 Sahai, *The Sterling Book of Essence of Indian Thought,* 2010.
63 *Ujjvalanilamani* and *Bhaktirasamrtasindhu* are the two main source books of Vaishnava philosophy of aesthetics. See Singh, "Abhinaya," 15–29.
64 Another north-eastern state of India. Assam, Arunachal Pradesh, Nagaland, Manipur, Mizoram, Tripura and Meghalaya grouped together are known as the Seven Sister states.
65 See Massey, *India's Dances,* 180–181.
66 Bandopadhay, "Manipuri Dance," 142.
67 Ibid.
68 The *Meitei* word for dance, "*jagoi,*" actually means "*chak-koi*" meaning "the going round of the ages." See Lightfoot, *Dance-rituals of Manipur, India,* 20.
69 Kothari, "New Directions in Indian Dance," 2008.
70 Singh, "Lai Haraoba," 30–34.
71 Ibid. See also, Singh, "Lai-haraoba: The Gods Rejoice," 11–18.
72 Narayan, *The Sterling Book of Indian Classical Dances,* 54.
73 See Ray, "Writing the Body," 130.
74 Bowers, "Dance and Opera in Manipur,"158.
75 Manipur also known as the "Switzerland of India" was known by many other names to its neighbours—the Shan or Pong called the area Cassay, the Burmese Kathe, and the Assamese Meklee. In 1762, the Britishers recorded it as the kingdom of Meckley. But soon the later rulers coined the Sanskrit term Manipureshwar or Manipur.
76 See Ray, "Boundaries Blurred?" 248.
77 Bandopadhay, "Manipuri Dance," 141.
78 Ibid., 142.
79 Doshi, "Editorial," 1988, iii.
80 Jhaveri, "The Raslila Performance Tradition of Manipur in Northeast India," 3.
81 Ibid., 1.
82 Ibid., 4
83 Ibid., 1.
84 Anand, "In Praise of Manipur," 2.
85 See Doshi, *Dances of Manipur,* 1989; Coorlawala, "The Classical Traditions of Odissi and Manipuri," 1993.
86 See Bandopadhay, "Dance: The Tool of Sanskritisation Process in Manipur," 2008.
87 Bandopadhay, "Manipuri Dance," 140–141.
88 For a discussion on *Meitei* festivals, see Parratt, *The Religion of Manipur,* 1980.
89 Jhaveri, "The Raslila Performance Tradition of Manipur in Northeast India," 5.
90 Chatterjea, "In Search of a Secular in Contemporary Indian Dance," 113–114.
91 See Singh, "Manipuri: Cause for Concern," 94. Since 1954, the JNMDA (Imphal), a constituent Unit of the Sangeet Natak Akademi (New Delhi), is still the premier institution for teaching of Manipuri Dance and Music and allied subjects like Thang Ta. The Akademi, besides setting up archives and publishing valuable research on Manipuri dance, has also organized inter/national festivals, seminars, and teaching sessions. See also Chatterjea, "Dance Research in India," 1996.
92 For a discussion on understanding the mythologies and religion of the various ethnic groups in Manipur, see Parratt, *The Religion of Manipur,* 1980; Phanjoubam, "Manipur: Fractured Land," 2005.
93 Bandopadhay, "Manipuri Dance," 140.

94 Hassan, "Understanding the Breakdown in North East India," 6.

95 Ibid., 7.

96 Parratt, *Wounded Land*, 126.

97 For a discussion on Indian political, cultural, religious and linguistic hegemony and resistance practices in Manipur, see Brara, *Politics, Society and Cosmology in India's North East*, 1998; Chelliah, "Linguistics Asserting Nationhood through Personal Name Choice," 2005; McDuie-Ra, *Debating Race in Contemporary India*, 2016.

98 *Kukis* (aka the Chin or the Zomi) and are related to the Tibeto-Burman tribal people. *Nagas* are an ethnic group associated to the North Eastern part of India especially Nagaland, Manipur, Arunachal Pradesh and Assam.

99 Bapat, *Re-scribing Tradition*, 71.

100 See Singh, "Manipuri: Cause for Concern," 98.

101 Banerjee, *Tagore's Mystique of Dance*, 2014. See also, Bandopadhay, *Manipuri Dance*, 2010.

102 Santidev Ghosh was a singer, dancer and an exponent of Manipuri dance at Tagore's university. See Ghosh, "Tagore and Manipuri Dances," 2011.

103 Banerjee, *Tagore's Mystique of Dance*, 2014.

104 See Thnag, "Rabindranath Tagore and His Influence in Bishnupriya Manipuri Society," 2008.

105 Sinha, "Rabindranath Tagore and the Bishnupriya Manipuri Community," 2011.

106 Ibid.

107 See Doshi, *Dances of Manipur*, 1989; See also Coorlawala, "The Classical Traditions of *Odissi* and *Manipuri*," 1993.

108 Ghosh, "Tagore and Manipuri Dances," 2011.

109 Ibid.

110 In 1970, Guru Amubi Singh was honoured with Padma Shri. Guru Amubi Singh for his contribution in creating a new *gharana* (school) that emphasized the *lasya* element and lyrical grace of Manipuri dance. Guru Bipin Singh founded Manipuri Nartanalaya in Kolkata, Mumbai and Imphal in 1972 to train a new generation of Manipuri dancers. He is regarded as the father of modern Manipuri dance and was awarded with many prestigious awards including National Sangeet Natak Academy. See Jhaveri and Devi, *Manipuri Nartana*, 1978; Jhaveri, *Guru Bipin Singh*, 1979; Kothari, "In Praise of Guru Bipin Singh," 2017.

111 Lightfoot, *Dance-Rituals of Manipur*, 1958.

112 Sebastian, "Reverse Pilgrimage," 260.

113 "Brouhaha over Bipin Singh," 15.

114 For a detailed analysis, see Chatterjea, "Contestations," 2013.

115 See Chatterjee, "Dance Research in India," 1996; Chakravorty, "From Interculturalism to Historicism," 108–119.

116 Srinivas, *Social Change in Modern India*, 56.

117 Phanjoubam, "Manipur: Fractured Land," 281.

118 Bandopadhay, "Dance: The Tool of Sanskritisation Process in Manipur," 2008.

119 Rojio, "Subdued Eloquence," 275–308.

120 For a discussion, see Sebastian, "Reverse Pilgrimage," 262; Rojio, "Subdued Eloquence," 275–308.

121 Sarwal, *The Dancing God*, 2020.

3 The Making of an Australian Impresario[1]

Louise Lightfoot (Louisa Mary Lightfoot), born in Yangery (near Warrnambool, Victoria) on 22 May 1902, was the fourth child and third daughter of Victorian-born parents Charles Lightfoot, a schoolteacher, and his wife Mary, née Graham.[2] She studied at the Catholic Ladies' College in East Melbourne, and in 1920 her father sent her to study Architecture at the University of Melbourne. In 1925, she was the first woman to earn a Diploma of Architecture in 1925.[3] While still a student, she began a four-year apprenticeship in the innovative architectural office of Walter Burley Griffin and Marion Mahony Griffin in Melbourne.[4] Louise remarks in her journal that although the Griffin's did not take apprentices, the famous architects made an exception for her.[5] In 1925, the Griffins moved to Castlecrag, Sydney, a new suburb intended as an ideal community in harmony with nature and culture.[6] Louise went too as a planner for the Griffins' office and as a companion to Marion.

Marion liked Louise as their interests and artistic activities aligned. Louise who was "tall, slender and graceful, striking in profile, beautiful rather than pretty" enjoyed dancing but could see no way to practise it as a profession.[7] She wrote: "Dancing at Carlyons, the Palais, hostess dances at Melba Hall and at the Beach Palais at Mornington! My boyfriends were recruited for dance-partners. My brother George, an excellent dancer, saw to it that I was never a wallflower."[8] Marion knew that Louise was fond of dancing and encouraged her natural talent and love of dance. Louise started learning "Eurhythmic" Greek dancing from Gertrude Sievers and found it "a little dull." On Anna Pavlova's first tour of Australia, in 1926, Louise found her fusion of classical technique and romantic emotion a "revelation."[9] She wrote about seeing Pavlova in the ballet *Giselle*: "She entered crossing the stage with a lily in her arms, and I was aware for a fraction of a second that I was in a sphere millions of miles above in a state of perfection."[10] Louise attended

DOI: 10.4324/9781003205203-4

Pavlova's presentations, especially of the Grand Russian Ballet, and dreamed of bringing the same to life in Australia.[11]

Through the Griffins, Louise met the Russian folk dancer Misha Burlakov, who had danced with Pavlova's tour.[12] She persuaded him to teach her the Russian *mazurka* and felt that her "real happiness started" when she danced with him in "peasant costume and red leather boots."[13] The "tall, willowy blonde" (Lightfoot) and the "strong, dark, jolly Russian" (Burlakov) danced at clubs, parties and soirees in the homes of artistic or wealthy Sydney-siders.[14] In her memoir, Marion notes how Louise and Misha made her Castlecrag soirees lively by arranging delightful programmes and bringing in the finest musical talent and visiting artists—"Louise went ahead with enthusiasm and industry, even with the surprising feats that Russians do."[15] The duo studied whatever forms of dance they could find and opened a dance school—Castlecrag Dancing School—teaching folk dances, also known as "character" dance and ballet, to a growing number of students. Soon, Louise and Misha established a ballet studio and large dance school at Circular Quay, Sydney out of which would grow their company—the First Australian Ballet.[16] In 1929, Louise and Misha, along with some of their pupils, began appearing in opera performances, dance recitals, and in various divertissements (Figure 3.1).[17] Louise's passion for dance was the driving force, complemented by Misha's dancing, mime and carpentry skills. They took every opportunity to "show their girls" on stage, and the students helped with costumes and scenery.

By March 1931, these early initiatives had developed enough for the Lightfoot-Burlakov school to be able to present their first classical dance production. Mary Louise Lightfoot notes that Rukmini Arundale, who had settled for some time in Sydney and was studying ballet at the Lightfoot-Burlakov studio, stimulated the idea of larger stage production for Lightfoot and Burlakov's students in which she would perform Pavlova's own creation *Indian Wedding* (along with *The Heart of Russia*). Indian Wedding was part of *Oriental Impressions*, a ballet created collaboratively by Uday Shankar and Pavlova.[18]

In November 1931, the First Australian Ballet presented a full ballet production—a two-act version of *Coppelia*.[19] Louise found a score of this ballet with extensive notes in J. C. Williamson's library.[20] Burlakov had seen Geneé's version and Louise was confident that she could design, produce and stage it. On 4 November 1931, at the Savoy Theatre, Sydney, Burlakov danced as Franz and the role of Swanhilda was shared between Jessie Cree (Act I) and Bertha Minoutochka (Act II). Louise had a difficult task, but she accomplished it, full of patriotism for Australia and a passion for art. Dance critic Valerie Lawson called the

Figure 3.1 (Left to Right) Louise Lightfoot and Misha Burlakov, dressed in black, performing in *Dance Brutale*.

Source: Photograph from the Louise Lightfoot Bequest, Monash University.

Photograph Courtesy: Music Archives of Monash University and Mary Louise Lightfoot.

First Australian Ballet "the starting block of professional ballet in Australia" and "an important building block for the professional companies to follow."[21] Mary Louise Lightfoot notes that the success of *Coppelia* soon prompted art and ballet lovers of Sydney to request repeat performances.[22] The company continued to perform regularly either in theatres or stages in the studio, at get-togethers or monthly meetings or fundraisers over the next decade. The Lightfoot-Burlakov studio also became a meeting place for visiting artists and dancers who attended classes at the studio and appeared in productions.[23] Louise was wholly immersed in teaching, ballet production, choreography, fundraising performances and financial management of the school. In 1936, Louise choreographed her version of *Petrouchka* at the Conservatorium, Sydney.[24]

Louise choreographed and produced several ballets a year in the 1930s, sometimes from memory—of productions seen in Australia—and often from descriptions in books and magazines. These included *Le Carnaval, Walpurgis Night, Les Sylphides, Le Spectre de la Rose, Scheherazade* and *Roksanda* (with a commissioned score from Roy Maling).[25] Lightfoot-Burlakov faced many difficulties in producing their works—ranging from threats of their studio buildings being pulled down to getting a copyright for musical scores and performance rights from overseas publishers and companies.[26] But Mary Louise Lightfoot observes that Louise was, through it all an exceptional teacher who would go to any lengths to inspire her students:

> Louise would manifest the educational and teaching background of her family in unusual ways throughout her life. She realised the great pool of talent in young people, inspired and promoted the appreciation of and active participation in the arts, especially dancing, in thousands of young people. She was a good teacher, a perfectionist, and would train dancers for the rest of her life.[27]

In 1937, to learn more about emerging dance styles, see performances of various ballet productions and to secure rights to perform a number of new ballets, Louise visited London and Paris with Misha. Nineteen-year-old Moya Beaver was persuaded by Louise to take charge of the dance school in her absence. Moya accepted the charge very reluctantly, and her father made sure that it was done legally, with a proper legal contract and not just a verbal agreement.[28] When the ship stopped in Bombay en route, Louise "fell under the spell of India."[29] She "purchased Indian dance costumes and socialised with handsome Indians on board, to the displeasure of the mostly white passengers."[30] Louise wrote:

> A very strange thing happened to me when we neared the shore of India and were standing on the deck watching the figures on the wharf grow more distinct … I had never had any special interest in India. My heart was set on Europe … I was amazed then at this great

flood of ecstasy which now came over me—ecstasy, anticipation, reverence, yearning, a bursting sensation as if my whole body would dissolve. I remember as we walked the streets of Bombay that day, I had the feeling of being "home at last."[31]

In Paris, the new home of Russian ballet, Louise and Misha found the coveted ballet scores. Louise also attended classes with famous Russian émigré teachers and experts in modern, Spanish and Hindu dances.[32] She wrote a letter to Beaver, sharing her feelings for India: "My mind was constantly going back to India, and I would have been run down many a time by dense traffic had it not been that Misha looked after me."[33] Louise was particularly impressed by the performances by the great Indian dancer and impresario Uday Shankar and his Indian Dance Company. In one of her letters to students in Sydney, Louise writes:

> One fine day a poster, printed in violet ink, appeared on Paris hoardings advertising. "UDAY SHANKAR ET SA COMPAGNIE DE DANSEUSES, DANSEURS ET MUSICIANS HINDOUS." Imagine my excitement! Ballet lessons were promptly "cut," and I immediately went to the particular theatre to find out more about this forthcoming event—Shankar was to give a season from the fourteenth to the twentieth of June at the Comedie des Theatre Champs Elysees. Now the greatest excitement of all—a ballet from India![34]

After seeing the show, Louise waited outside the dressing rooms, waiting to see Uday Shankar. She says:

> Later, at my interview with this handsome Indian, I requested some lessons in Kathakali. He made a statement that I doubted at the time, but since learnt was true.
>
> "I really know very little about Indian dancing," he said. "I must myself go back to India and study. Then how I can teach you?"
>
> But I was not to be put off so easily.
>
> Finally, he said, "Sometimes you can come and see me and I may have time to show you a few gestures." I came the next day and had a chat with the Manager, but I could not see Shankar.[35]

Although Louise was unable to get lessons from Shankar, her co-artist

Madhavan gave her the address of a school in Kerala for training in Kathakali.

Louise told the *Woman's Weekly* that she intended to create a new Indian ballet on her return to Australia.[36] In order to bring more authenticity to her ballet, Louise got off the ship in Bombay to study Indian dance. Mary Louise Lightfoot observes that this was "strange for the time" as "[w]omen didn't travel much, especially on their own, and the 'Dark Continent' of India, though a part of the British Empire was an unusual destination for a single white Australian woman."[37] In her diary, Louise writes:

> My first introduction to traditional Indian dance was at the Fellowship School, showing "Manipuri" movements—lovely, graceful things of which I had seen nothing in Shankar's program, and very different from the virile Kathakali movements.[38]

Louise spent more than five months in India where she again met Rukmini Devi Arundale in Adyar. Rukmini Devi's Kalakshetra Dance Academy, established in 1936, had established her as one of the key players—"an educated and cultural artiste from outside the ranks of the professional dancers"—in the Bharatanatyam revival in India.[39] For the "educated and cultured" audiences, Rukmini Devi purified *sadhir* dance and replaced the sensual and carnal moves with innovative religious emphasis. Louise later recalled:

> After a couple of weeks, Rukmini came to watch my lesson. Knowing how amusing it can be to see an Oriental woman imitating a sylph. I could just imagine how comic I, a Westerner, looked when imitating a *devadasi*, so I quite forgave Rukmini's smiles. She was surprised that I could learn so much when I could not converse with the teacher.[40]

Louise returned to Australia from India reluctantly.

Louise started training her students to showcase the story of Bhagwan Krishna on stage. In May 1938, Lightfoot-Burlakov produced their last joint recital—Louise's own "authentic Hindu style movement" version of *The Blue God* with Indian costumes, ornaments and recorded *Vedic mantra* chants sourced from India—at the NSW Conservatorium of Music.[41] Louise notes in her journal:

> Only seven out of all our students mastered the Bharata Natya movements sufficiently to satisfy me, and these girls took the part of

temple-devadasis, while about eighteen young girls danced Manipuri movements in inter-weaving circles, as offering bearers. Others joined in the crowd scenes. Our young men, eight of them, danced as religious fanatics, while a promising young student Gordon Hamilton danced the role of the *Blue God*.[42]

During the various shows of the *Blue God* in Sydney and Canberra, Louise was once again tempted to go back to India. She wrote:

> One day as I was idly turning the pages of a "Four Arts" magazine I had purchased the day of my first arrival in India, my eyes were suddenly focussed on a photograph printed therein—a photo of a school building. Underneath was written: "Keralakalamandalam, Cochin State, under the direction of the well-known Kerala Poet Vallathol."

> I wired my friend in India for details of the address of this famous man, and back came the information within a few days. I remembered how surprised I was that the long name of the school had been allowed in the wire as one word. I wrote to the school at once asking all about it, and whether I would be permitted to study there. A reply soon came from the secretary, Mukund Raja, and I was informed I would be most welcome at this interesting school.[43]

Louise did not inform Misha about this development.[44] After *The Blue God*, Louise dissolved her partnership with Misha, packed her bags and returned to India—to the Malabar Coast (Kerala)—to find Kathakali.[45] Louise felt a bit relieved at this decision:

> … After the show, I announced my intended departure, and our students were not very surprised.

> I booked a passage to India in the Stratheden leaving in October. Misha received the news surprisingly well. Of late he had begun to cherish ideas of reigning supreme in a school. I was never quite sure whether he meant it or not. Regarding my departure, I was unable to give him any idea of how long I would be absent, and I left it entirely to him to make his own arrangements during that time.[46]

Misha continued the First Australian Ballet with the assistance of Barbara McDonnell, one of the company dancers and a teacher at the school.[47] The First Australian Ballet disbanded in the 1950s and Misha continued to teach at his own school until his death in 1965.[48]

In 1938, Louise arrived at the Kerala Kalamandalam and recorded her first observation thus:

> I hope anyone visiting the land of Kathakali will arrive at his destination in the dawn, as I did. Apart from the particular loveliness of dawn in that country, it was the dawn of a new kind of life that will never be forgotten. Maybe the arduous journey I had experienced made my arrival all the sweeter. Certainly, it was the happiest dawn I had ever known, and it was filled with a sense of "coming home."[49]

Here, she adapted quickly to the Kerala village life: "Friends have sometimes wondered how I adapted myself so quickly to Indian village life. Perhaps adventure was already in my blood because my four grandparents were all adventurers in the 'new' land of Australia."[50] Louise's teacher Kunju Nair did not speak English and used Sanskrit words to teach Kathakali. A fellow student named Krishnamurty, who knew a bit of English, was appointed as an interpreter for Louise. Every day, she would wake up at 6 am to get ready for her 8 am training in "a cool, palm-thatched shed."[51] She also made a point to watch as many Kathakali performances as possible by accompanying the Kalamandalam troupe. Soon she needed money to survive in Kerala and started looking for some work to sustain herself:

> Having savoured a taste of Kathakali, I decided to follow its call and settle in India near Kerala. I ascertained that the nearest hill-station that had European colleges was at Ootacamund in the Nilgiri ranges above Kerala. There I would try to earn a living by teaching, so that I could continue my studies under a Kathakali master.[52]

Apart from studying Kathakali, Krishnamurty encouraged Louise to use her skills in troupe management to establish her own troupe of Kathakali dancers.

In 1939, Krishnamurty introduced Louise to a very talented young dancer at Kalamandalam. Ananda Shivaram studied as well as tutored Kathakali dance at this institution. Louise noted that as a substitute teacher for Kunju Nair and Madhavan, Shivaram was hopeless and an utter disappointment.[53] But when she saw Shivaram essaying the role of Krishna in a dance-drama based on the Indian epic *Mahabharata*, she says,

> Soon after seeing Shivaram in Kathakali, I felt a wish to stretch out my hand and capture that little creature. Then I would always have

Kathakali in the palm of my hand. I could turn on happiness any time, I thought—as if we could capture what is in a bird![54]

Louise persuaded Shivaram to experiment, to create shorter versions of dance-dramas, and to adapt ancient Kathakali works to modern tastes with her Hindu Dance Group in Australia. Louise and Shivaram, with the help of Stella Kramrisch, a well-known American curator and interpreter of Indian art and the key figure behind the Indian Society of Oriental Art, performed at the Ramakrishna Mission in the late 1930s. Louise produced a shorter version of Kathakali, much to audiences' amazement.

> We trimmed the Kathakali performance down to two and a half-hours for the English and Bengali audiences—just the highlights. Stella Kramrisch (the moving spirit of the Indian Society of Oriental Art) and I were careful to see that lamp oil was not kept on stage in a kerosene tin, that followers did not stand near the stage or walk across, that bell and costume strings were neatly tied. Fortunately, no attempt was made to alter the traditional lighting, setting or costumes.[55]

These "presentations used a similar format to Louise's Australian productions."[56] Rather than having all-night performances of major Hindu epics, Louise and Shivaram mixed short scenes from different epics. Their other strategy was to include different folk and classical dances. Considering the highly codified performance associated with Kathakali, this experimentation was surprising, but ultimately well-received by Kathakali lovers and critics.[57]

Over the next half-decade, Louise lived in Kerala and Tamil Nadu, learning the different techniques of the sacred dance styles Kathakali and Bharatanatyam.[58] She wrote a detailed account of her visit and life in India. This was published later in a book of her adventures, entitled "*Adventures in Kathakali.*" Louise and Shivaram moved to Madras from where she continued writing in newspapers on various topics, teaching Ballet and organizing local tours for Shivaram as a publicist.

Despite critical acclaim coming their way, Louise and Shivaram found that earning money was a problem. Louise got in touch with Uday Shankar's brother, Rajendra, with a request to accept Shivaram as a resident performer at Shankar's newly opened India Culture Centre in Almora, North India.[59] After visiting the centre, Louise thought of taking admission as a private student for beginner's classes in Bharatanatyam but was refused by the secretary of the institute: "No European students are being admitted to the Centre for five years. You may apply for special permission if you wish and your application will go before the committee."[60] After a few days, Louise was invited to appear before an interview board consisting of an American administrator and Uday Shankar. Louise explained her case and the reason behind her interest in taking admission at the Centre. Shankar asked Louise: "You might perhaps teach Indian dancing there [in Australia] when you go back, and produce Indian ballet?"[61] Louise responded positively and Shankar refused Louise admission—he did not want a repeat of the "dreadful things Le Meri had done in New York."[62] While Shivaram stayed inside the Centre, Louise managed to get accommodation outside and continued writing and making plans for Shivaram. As Shivaram got busy in his new roles and learning, Louise got a letter from Asoka (aka Ernst Rubener), a German dancer based in India.[63] Inspired by the work and fame of Uday Shankar, Asoka had travelled to India in the 1930s to learn Bharatanatyam. He invited Louise to join him and organize a tour for him and his partner. Shivaram could not believe that Louise had decided to leave him alone in Almora and move to Bombay.

While Louise was in Bombay, she saw the effects of World War II in India. Foreigners, especially Germans, were rounded up and sent to camps as enemy aliens by the British Indian Army. Asoka and his German friends were taken away too, and Louise was out of work again. Nevertheless, she was not ready to leave India. Louise moved into a hostel run by nuns. To earn a living in Bombay, she started giving radio talks on a 1:35 pm broadcast called "Do You Know, Madame?" and writing on art for the *Bombay Chronicle* for a very small fee.[64]

By the end of August 1940, Louise was fed-up with her gigs at the radio and the newspaper. She wanted to get back in action with Kathakali. While on bed rest because of a high fever, she received a surprise visit from dancer Ram Gopal. With the support of wealthy patrons, Ram Gopal had been to Japan, the United States, France and Britain.[65] However, the war had put a stop to his foreign tours and he was in Bombay to scout for talent to form a new dance troupe in Bangalore. He offered Louise a role as assistant organizer, free tuition in Indian dance and Rupees fifty a month as pocket money. Louise accepted Ram Gopal's offer and was happy to go back to pursuing her passion. In her excitement and happiness, however, she did not forget Shivaram:

> By evening Ram Gopal arrived with a taxi and soon I was lying comfortably in a first-class compartment, sipping very hot cocoa and regaling the amused Ram with the story of Sister's appearance at my door. Then it was his turn to talk, and how he could talk! He

described how he danced and danced as one possessed. I lay back satisfied that I had found my real work at last. Perhaps Shivaram would help us one day with his Kathakali.[66]

The next few years were full of adventure with Ram Gopal and his troupe. Louise wrote to J. C. Williamson's theatrical firm about bringing Ram Gopal's Indian dance troupe to Australia. But the firm thought that at that point in time, bringing an authentic Indian dance and music troupe "might not be appreciated."[67]

Soon, adventures with Ram Gopal came to end with a bitter fight. Louise, who was also once again trying to branch out as a Ballet teacher in India, did not disclose her relation with Ram Gopal's Indian dance school during one of her lectures at a leading European Girls' School. Ram Gopal was furious to read newspaper reports about Louise's talk, which made no mention of his name or school. Louise apologized to Ram Gopal, left his school and moved into a guest-house run by a Quaker woman in the Bangalore Cantonment area. After this bitter experience with Ram Gopal, Shivaram was once again in Louise's thoughts:

> I dumped my trunks gratefully and opened up a large tube-like parcel I had just received in the post. It contained an oil painting of Shivaram by an American living not far from the Shankar Cultural Centre in Almora. I nailed the canvas up on the wall. The pose was stiff, the head turned sideways. It would have been fine if the head had suddenly turned and smiled.[68]

In Bangalore, Louise was once again actively teaching ballet to English and Anglo-Indian children at the residence of an English Colonel.[69]

Louise was thrilled by the whole experience of learning Kathakali—involving poetry, song, acting and dance—and she was constantly appealing to both the British in India to appreciate Indian dance and to Indian parents to allow their sons and daughters to dance. While she learnt dancing and organized tours for Indian artists at Kalamandalam, Louise was also busy publishing in Indian, British and Australian newspapers and magazines regarding Hindu dance, her journey to Kalamandalam, the Indian way of life and other socio-cultural issues.[70]

In 1940, she published an "International Appeal of the Ballet" in *The Hindu* (February 11):

> We can help in the cause of art by making a fuss of these artists and their splendid work, which will soon make Indian Ballet a powerful influence on the whole world of Ballet. We are preparing the

world—so we hope—for an international understanding, and there is nothing more completely international in its appeal than Ballet.[71]

In 1946, Louise published a piece on Kathakali in an Australian newspaper, *The Argus* (31 July 1946), titled "Two Thousand Years of Rhythm." She writes:

> Educated young women, including the daughter of the first woman member [of] the Legislative Assembly, are studying Kathakali. Even though they haven't much knowledge of it yet, they are enthralling the sophisticated, cinema-loving audiences of India's big cities.[72]

Louise realized at a very early stage that Kathakali would never be "adopted entirely by Western dancers," and audiences, because it "wouldn't suit them."[73] In addition to the time and dedication needed to be a trained Kathakali artist (which also explained why few Indians were not born to the art and very very few Western dancers were pursuing it), Kathakali's aesthetic was wholly alien to the West.

> [W]e are so close to India here, we know comparatively nothing of the art of this great ancient land. It is not our fault exactly. We are not educated to think that there is anything of particular interest for us in this neighbouring country.[74]

Therefore, it was best to infuse the Indian rhythms of this symbolic art with Western dance and vice versa. Here, Louise's knowledge and training in architecture, sculpture and painting helped her in the elaborate planning of costumes, ornaments and stage design. Nevertheless, this experimentation could not have been possible without the active support of Ananda Shivaram—Louise's teacher, friend and star artist.

Louise, the first Australian and the first Western woman to study this art, immersed herself first in studying Kathakali in theory, the traditional, all-night dance-drama performed in Hindu temples. She soon became a great publicist of Indian dance troupes and soloists by organizing tours for troupes in South India and Ceylon (Sri Lanka). To support herself and the work, she taught classical ballet to children of the British Raj. She also worked with filmmaker K. Subramanyam[75] at Madras (Chennai) and published her perspective pieces widely in the Indian press. Subramanyam offered a generous salary and engaged Louise as his Director of Art and Publicity at the Madras United Artist Corporation. The film was entitled "Narthana Murali" (the Dancing Krishna). Keeping in mind the theme and story of the film, Louise was hopeful that Shivaram would get the leading role in the film as Bhagwan Krishna and it would be of advantage for her to introduce him to Australia—as an Indian dancer and film star. However, Louise's talented friend, the modest Shivaram, was relegated to the background behind the flamboyant and domineering dancer Gopinath. Louise was angry but continued with her job with Subramaniam. She now had one goal in mind: to save enough to take Shivaram abroad.[76] The production problems led this film to be shelved and soon the artists and most of the people involved in filming resigned, including Louise.

In September 1945, as soon as World War II ended, Louise sailed for Australia, intent on bringing Hindu dance to her country. She was a bit anxious about the reception of a Hindu dancer in White Australia. Louise wrote:

> How would Australian people appreciate this living temple fresco I was bringing to them? Would they be interested in a Museum of Temple Art tucked into a little dark man? Would they realise the importance of it all, and link it with plans for future world-peace?
>
> Much depended on me as Impresario and would-be missionary of Hindu Culture. I began negotiations for a permit to bring my treasure to White Australia. I knew better than to ask financial help from either India or Australia—that might delay me many years and end in disappointment. Shivaram must come alone.[77]

When Louise's mother heard that she was bringing a Hindu dancer to Australia, she sent a message, "On no account bring a coloured gentleman with you! You would be very much misunderstood."[78] The British Resident in Madras expressed similar feelings. Shivaram told Mary Louise Lightfoot that on seeing the big English Resident, he tried to hide behind Louise. The Resident was not at all encouraging and told Louise coldly: "Only cricketers from India go to Australia. I've never heard of any artist from India going there."[79] But Louise was adamant and Shivaram was loyal to the cause. Louise contacted the Indian High Commissioner in Australia, Sir Raghunath Paranjpye, and through his request, Shivaram got permission to stay in Australia on a six-month visa. But their troubles were not yet over. It took years to complete the necessary paperwork, birth certificates, police verification and passport for Shivaram. Louise wrote:

> Likewise, the P&O shipping agents in Bombay and Calcutta had no hopes of getting us passages to Australia because there were eight

hundred names ahead of ours on the list. They thought it might be a year before we got away! Fares were still at First Class rates only.[80]

During the waiting period, Louise travelled to Calcutta to join Shivaram and study Bharatanatyam from Ellappa—a renowned teacher from Madras who had trained many *devadasis*. In Calcutta, Shivaram and his partner were to perform with Neena Maya, who was trained in Russian Ballet and performed in theatres of China, Japan, Java, Burma and Malaya.[81] Neena's patron left for London and wrote back that he won't be able to return to India anytime soon. So, Neena requested him to organize her tour with Shivaram in London. Louise recalls:

> We began to arrange beautiful costumes for Shivaram's proposed appearances with her in London. A photographer called and took pictures of the pair in their Bharata Natya costumes.[82]

This proposed tour never eventuated and because of a sudden cancellation on a cargo ship bound for Australia, Louise got a ticket to travel home, a chance she may not get for another six months.[83] On board, Louise thought of how Shivaram wept when she told him about her impending journey. She also thought about Rajkumar Priyagopal Singh—a Manipuri dancer—who was planning to host Louise in Imphal, Manipur, so he could eventually travel abroad with her as impresario. She wrote:

> Oh, frustrated Indian dancers, born for the Creator Brahma's plan of showering righteousness to the world! Who in these times will help you to fulfil your vocation? The boat's engine chugged away while my new role as a missionary of Hindu Art rose before me. The loved land of India was fading, while I saw as in a dream, my work, remembering to add the words "God Willing."[84]

Mary Louise Lightfoot writes that the journey back to Australia (May 1946) with this profound sense of purpose and dedication to Hindu dance was the end of Louise's unpublished manuscript of her adventures.

In Melbourne, Louise successfully started preparing the public to receive her "treasure"—by publishing extensively on Hindu dance art in Australian newspapers and magazines, teaching selected Australian ballet students Indian dance and giving public talks at the Theosophical Society and at Ballet clubs.[85]

> Louise spoke of discovering Indian dance, an ancient and perfect art, though in danger of extinction; of Indian dance being more than

entertainment, being considered an approach to God; and how the Hindu temple was the home of all arts.[86]

In addition, Mary Louise Lightfoot notes that Louise also started networking with people running art festivals and shows in Australia. Meanwhile, in India, Shivaram had left Neena Maya's troupe and joined Army Entertainment. As an entertainer for the troops, Shivaram performed in Singapore until the shipping routes were clear after the end of the war.[87]

In March 1947, Louise finally brought Shivaram to Australia and became his publicist, painstakingly organizing, publicizing and explaining the art form to audiences through her well-researched lectures and commentaries. She, as planned, single-handedly controlled myriad other tasks associated with event management. Mary Louise Lightfoot recalls a conversation with Shivaram where he explained his first experience of landing in Melbourne:

> Shivaram's ship [*SS Marella*] sailed into Melbourne on the morning of March 20th 1947. The wharf seemed empty to him, compared to Indian wharves. Louise and Ruth met him at the pier, with some members of the press and a representative of the Australian-Indian Association. It was the first visit of an Indian dancer or artist to Australia. Up till then, no manager had been prepared to bring Uday Shankar's troupe to Australia, mostly because of the financial commitment needed, and because people were not at all accustomed to the music or dance of Asia.[88]

Shivaram arrived dressed in a grey *shenvani* (traditional Indian long coat) attracting the attention of photojournalists eager to capture him. By the end of his visit, he was a star, just as Louise had wished. He was liked by everyone—the first Indian Kathakali artist to tour Australia (Figure 3.2).[89]

Shivaram, then in his early thirties, performed in all the major Australian cities: Melbourne, Sydney, Brisbane, Adelaide, Hobart and Perth. The Australian media overwhelmingly characterized him as an "exotic Hindu temple dancer." His first major show was organized at the National Theatre in Melbourne, under the patronage of the Indian High Commissioner to Australia, Sir Raghunath Purushottam Paranjpye. The Indian media saw this collaboration between Shivaram, Lightfoot and other Australian Ballet artists as a much-awaited "cultural union between the Orient and the Occident."[90]

The extensive notes, commentaries, explanations and interpretation of the art of *Kathakali* that Louise provided for the public came in as a

Figure 3.2 (Left to Right) Ananda Shivaram, dressed in traditional Indian *sherwani*, received by Louise Lightfoot at Port Melbourne on board *SS Marella*, 1947.

Source: Photograph from the Louise Lightfoot Bequest, Monash University.

Photograph Courtesy: Music Archives of Monash University and Mary Louise Lightfoot.

"valuable aid." Drawing on her own experience, she made the "fascinating grace, spectacular beauty and historical charm" all plainly understandable.[91] Amazed by the hard work and time-consuming makeup technique, the correspondent of the *Sun Women's Magazine* (9 April 1947) remarked that Shivaram had "brought most of the make-up components with him, and was preparing them in the ancient Indian style by grinding coloured stones with a pestle, and mixing them with coconut oil."[92] Louise and Shivaram's experimentation in the fusion of Eastern and Western practices and making a classical Indian form accessible to uninitiated audiences was an overwhelming success. Audiences and critics were bowled over by the eloquence, expressiveness, and range of characterization of Shivaram's Kathakali performances. After his first tour, Shivaram attracted attention from journalists and public alike, in Australia, New Zealand and Fiji, as a picturesque figure with shoulder-length hair—a "short, slightly built man with flowing black hair, dressed in his national costume of all white."[93] The critical consensus was that the audiences had viewed the ancient temple dances as if on a "magic carpet" ride.[94]

Australian connoisseurs of ballet were "profoundly interested" and "pleasantly impressed" with Shivaram's "original demonstrations."[95] Comparing the dance style of Shivaram with that of the American modern dancer Ted Shawn, Seymour wrote in *The Mail*: "… the most marvellous thing in Shivaram's dancing is his virility, which makes such a deep impression … it unleashes before us a power and vitality completely masculine and astonishingly thrilling."[96] Alan Seymour notes that during her stay in India, the "religious tradition" and the "deep spiritual content of Indian dance" had had "an over-whelming effect" on Louise and she had "absorbed its technique and emotional content" in her own presentations.[97] According to Moya Beaver, no Australian woman had done this before.[98] Seymour also notes, not at all surprised, that Louise displayed that quintessential Australian trait of "initiative." He writes that "… unlike many Australians in the theatre world who have gone abroad and forgotten to come back, she has devotedly, and with passionate sincerity, attempted to bring something of culture, enlightenment, and international goodwill to the Australian people."[99] Louise devoted her considerable talents—experiences drawn from promoting ballet in Australia—and energy to promoting Hindu or Indian classical dance. Seeing Louise's dedication towards promoting Kathakali, Vallathol Narayana Menon, the great poet of Malabar and the founder of Kerala Kalamandalam, bestowed upon Louise the fond title of "Kathakali's Australian mother."[100]

Louise's discovery, Shivaram, was on his way to becoming an international star. A rich Indian-origin business owner invited Louise and Shivaram to Fiji and they were "put up" at the iconic Grand Pacific Hotel (Figure 3.3).[101] On their return to Melbourne, however, Louise and Shivaram were told by the officers of the immigration department that Shivaram's visa was meant for Australia and his Fiji tour had led to its cancellation. On Louise's request, the officials granted a few weeks' stay to Shivaram to make arrangements for his travel back to India. But in any case, Shivaram was now ready to move on and explore Europe. Mary Louise Lightfoot notes that Louise and Shivaram boarded *Marseilles* from Freemantle bound for Ceylon and Bombay. They did not get down at Bombay as planned and moved on to London to showcase India's new cultural ambassador—"Instead of returning then to India, something told me to go to London. From 1947 to 1950, Shivaram performed in Australia, Fiji, New Zealand and England with Louise as his trusted impresario.[102] In the 1950s, Shivaram wanted to rest after years of touring continuously and Louise was interested in learning other traditional dance forms of India, especially the folk culture of Manipur.[103] This was her chance to popularize a form older than the Hindu traditions—Manipuri dance.

Figure 3.3 (Sitting in the centre, from left to right) Ruth Bergner, Ananda Shivaram and Louise Lightfoot photographed with a group of dancers and show organizers in Suva, Fiji, 1950.

Source: Photograph from the Louise Lightfoot Bequest, Monash University.

Photograph Courtesy: Music Archives of Monash University and Mary Louise Lightfoot.

Notes

1 Parts of this chapter have appeared as "Introduction" in *Louise Lightfoot in Search of India: An Australian Dancer's Experience* (2017) and as "The Australian mother of Kathakali" in *The Dancing God: Staging Hindu Dance in Australia* (2020). Published here with the permission of Cambridge Scholars Publishing and Routledge.

2 To compile Louise's biography, I have used material from Lightfoot and Quartly, "Lightfoot, Louisa Mary (1902–1979)," 2005; Lightfoot, "Lightfoot, Louise," 2008; NLA Dance, "Indian Dance in Australia," 2010; Brissenden and Glennon, *Australia Dances*, 2010; Lightfoot, *Lightfoot Dancing*, 2015.

3 See Lightfoot and Quartly, "Lightfoot, Louisa Mary (1902–1979)," 2005.

4 Walter Burley Griffin was an American architect and landscape architect, who is best known for his role in designing Canberra, Australia's capital city. Griffin visited Lucknow (India) in the 1930s and was inspired by the architecture and culture of India. He died of peritonitis in early 1937, five days after gallbladder surgery at King George's Hospital in Lucknow, and was buried in Christian Cemetery in Lucknow.

5 Lightfoot, *Lightfoot Dancing*, Chapter 6.
6 Castlecrag was originally planned by Walter Burley Griffin, who named the suburb after a towering crag of rock overlooking Middle Harbour, known locally as Edinburgh Castle.
7 See Lightfoot and Quartly, "Lightfoot, Louisa Mary (1902–1979)," 2005.
8 Lightfoot, *Lightfoot Dancing*, Chapter 6.
9 See Lightfoot and Quartly, "Lightfoot, Louisa Mary (1902–1979)," 2005.
10 Lightfoot, *Lightfoot Dancing*, Chapter 7.
11 Pavlova's company presented nineteen ballet pieces including *Don Quixote*, *The Magic Flute* and *Autumn Leaves*. See Ibid.
12 Misha (or Mischa) Burlakov was born in Ukraine and came to Australia in 1913. He had performed national and folk dances for various clubs and appeared in classical ballet recitals in NSW. See Brissenden and Glennon, *Australia Dances*, 82.
13 See Lightfoot and Quartly, "Lightfoot, Louisa Mary (1902–1979)," 2005.
14 See Lightfoot, "Lightfoot, Louise," 2008.
15 Griffin, *The Magic of America*, 2007; Lightfoot, *Lightfoot Dancing*, Chapter 7.
16 "The First Australian Ballet (1929–1950)," 2010.
17 See Brissenden and Glennon, *Australia Dances*, 82–83.
18 Lightfoot, *Lightfoot Dancing*, 2015.
19 *Coppelia* is a comic ballet based on two stories by E. T. A. Hoffmann, namely *Der Sandmann* (The Sandman) and *Die Puppe* (The Doll).
20 See Brissenden and Glennon, *Australia Dances*, 82.
21 Quoted in Lightfoot, "Lightfoot, Louise," 2008.
22 Lightfoot, *Lightfoot Dancing*, Chapter 9.
23 The cost of attending a dance class at their studio was around one to two shillings. See Ibid.
24 *Petrushka* (*Petrouchka*) is a ballet that tells the story of a Russian traditional puppet Petrushka, who is made of straw, with a bag of sawdust as his body, but who comes to life and develops emotions.
25 See Brissenden and Glennon, *Australia Dances*, 83.
26 Ibid.
27 Lightfoot, *Lightfoot Dancing*, Chapter 9.
28 Ibid., Chapter 10.
29 See Lightfoot, "Lightfoot, Louise," 2008.
30 Ibid.
31 Quoted in Gibson, "Dancer's Dream Lives on," 1999.
32 See Lightfoot, "Lightfoot, Louise," 2008.
33 Lightfoot, *Lightfoot Dancing*, Chapter 2.
34 Ibid.
35 Ibid.
36 See Lightfoot and Quartly, "Lightfoot, Louisa Mary (1902–1979)," 2005.
37 Lightfoot, *Lightfoot Dancing*, Chapter 1.
38 Ibid., Chapter 11.
39 Quoted in Katrak, *Contemporary Indian Dance*, 30.
40 Lightfoot, *Lightfoot Dancing*, Chapter 11.
41 Louise used Manipuri dance steps learned from Rajkumar Priyagopal Singh's father Maharaja Surjaboro Singh to create the choreography of *The Blue God*.
42 Lightfoot, *Lightfoot Dancing*, Chapter 11.
43 Ibid.

44 Ibid.
45 Involving the unfolding of stories in dance or dance-drama, Kathakali originated from *Krishnanattam* (Sanskrit plays in praise of Bhagwan Krishna) and *Ramanattam* or Attakatha (Malayalam plays in praise of Bhagwan Rama) in the coastal state of Kerala during the seventeenth century. Kathakali does not include any onstage dialogue at all and is noted chiefly for being an all-male domain (even female roles are played by men). The variety and range of characters from noble heroes to demons and religious themes and stories concerning the victory of good over evil are drawn from *Mahabharata*, the *Ramayana*, and the *Puranas*.
46 Lightfoot, *Lightfoot Dancing*, Chapter 11.
47 Brissenden and Glennon, *Australia Dances*, 84.
48 Ibid.
49 Lightfoot, *Lightfoot Dancing*, Chapter 12.
50 Ibid.
51 Ibid.
52 Ibid., Chapter 13.
53 Madhavan worked with Uday Shankar and was bringing Western ideas of dancing, particularly of having a key female partner on stage. Later, he was dismissed as a teacher from Kerala Kalamandalam for misconduct. See Lightfoot, *Lightfoot Dancing*, Chapter 14.
54 Ibid.
55 Lightfoot, *Lightfoot Dancing*, Chapter 14.
56 Ibid., Chapter 15.
57 For a discussion on experimentation in Kathakali, see Fischer-Lichte, *Dionysus Resurrected*, 2013; Zarrilli, *Kathakali Dance Drama*, 2000.
58 See Lightfoot and Quartly, "Lightfoot, Louisa Mary (1902–1979)," 2005.
59 Despite the extraordinary reach and patronage offered by well-known artists, writers and political figures such as Michael Chekhov, John Martin, Nehru, Romain Rolland, Sir William Rothenstein, Leopold Stokowski, and Tagore, Shankar's Centre lasted only four years. See Vertinsky and Ramachandran. "Uday Shankar and the Dartington Hall Trust," 298.
60 Lightfoot, *Lightfoot Dancing*, Chapter 17.
61 Ibid.
62 Ibid.
63 See Kumar, "Meet Sujata and Asoka, the Indo-German dancers who charmed Hollywood in the 1950s," 2016.
64 Ibid.
65 Ibid., Chapter 19.
66 Ibid., Chapter 18.
67 Ibid., Chapter 19.
68 Ibid., Chapter 20.
69 Ibid.
70 Ibid., Chapter 15.
71 Lightfoot, "International Appeal of the Ballet," 1940.
72 Lightfoot, "Two Thousand Years of Rhythm," 16.
73 Ibid.
74 Lightfoot, "Explanation of Items by Miss Lightfoot's Hindu Dance Group," 1947.

75 K. Subramanyam (1904–1971) was an Indian film director of the 1930s and 1940s. He is considered a key figure behind the establishment of the Tamil film industry.

76 Ibid., Chapter 24.

77 Ibid., Chapter 25.

78 Lightfoot, "A Few Stories of Shivaram by His Australian Impresario," 1947.

79 Lightfoot, *Lightfoot Dancing*, Chapter 25.

80 Ibid.

81 Ibid.

82 Ibid.

83 Ibid.

84 Ibid.

85 Ibid., Chapter 26.

86 Ibid.

87 Ibid.

88 Ibid.

89 See "Hindu Dancer Astounds with Muscle Control," 1950; Artlover Madras, "Ananda Shivaram: India's Cultural Ambassador," 3; Broinowski, *The Yellow Lady*, 1996.

90 Artlover Madras, "Ananda Shivaram: India's Cultural Ambassador," 3.

91 "Indian Dancer: Entrancing Display by Shivaram," 10.

92 "Friendly Indian Likes Us," 1947.

93 "Temple Dancer Says Fiji an Indian's Paradise," 4.

94 "Dancers' Art Delights," 5.

95 "Indian Dancer: Entrancing Display by Shivaram," 10.

96 Seymour, "Presenting Louise Lightfoot," 51.

97 Ibid.

98 See Beaver, "Interview with Michelle Potter," 1994.

99 Seymour, "Presenting Louise Lightfoot," 51.

100 "Australian *Kathakali* Artiste Dead," *The Indian Express*, 2 July 1979.

101 Ibid.

102 As Louise's friendship and respect for Shivaram's work grew, she focused particularly on arranging performances for Shivaram (1947, Australia; 1948, London and Fiji; 1949, Australia and New Zealand; 1952, Japan; 1953, Canada; 1954, 1955, and 1960–1963, U.S.; 1957, Australia and Indonesia; 1959 and 1963–1967, Canada; 1974, Australia).

103 Lightfoot, *Lightfoot Dancing*, Chapter 28.

4   The Prince and his Master Drummer[1]

In February 1951, Louise Lightfoot, then 49 years old, "sailed straight to Bombay" to meet Rajkumar Priyagopal Singh (Rajkumar Priya Gopal Sana). It was always a part of her plan to return to India one day, to just visit Manipur and learn Manipuri dance.

> I always planned to return to India one day and visit that far-distant land of Manipur, … So when my Kathakali artist Shivaram went home, I sailed straight to Bombay and luckily found there that same Manipuri dancer who had delighted me in Calcutta some years before.[2]

Louise had previously met and seen Priyagopal, an expert Manipuri dancer, who performed in Calcutta [Kolkata] at Santiniketan, Gurudev Rabindranath Tagore's institute. She had also taken some dance lessons with his guru and father, Maharaja Surjaboro Singh (Surjaboro Sana, Suraj Barasing and Suja Bara Sana)—a renowned dancer and musician himself—in the late 1930s and early 1940s, while she was arranging tours for various South Indian artistes, especially Shivaram. Following a visit to Santiniketan with Shivaram, she remarked:

> After dumping my belongings at the YWCA, I made arrangements for tuition from a Manipuri Guru, Surjaboro Singh of Imphal. He was giving lessons at the rooms of the Indian society of Oriental Art. The Guru was a dear little man with Mongolian-type features ….

> One evening I went to see a recital of "Manipuri and Kamrupi" dances by men from Assam. The surprise of it was Priyagopal. He appeared in two solos substituting for an absent dancer. He proved to be a magnificent dancer and quite stole the show. His sword dance left us breathless with its cat-like and incredibly swift

DOI: 10.4324/9781003205203-5

movements. His postures, supported on one leg with the knee bent to an incredible extent, were utterly novel to me, and yet so like then Indian sculptures of what I had previously considered impossible dance positions. He was delighted by my enthusiasm and requested me to take him for "my troupe."[3]

After this performance, Louise and Shivaram returned to Kerala to take charge of Kalamandalam's troupe.[4] Although she wanted to "snap" Priyagopal then, her focus till the 1950s remained solely on Kathakali. In a 1951 article "In Search of Manipur," Louise wrote: "I could not forget the Manipuri Dance."[5] Priyagopal saw her outside his apartment flat in Bombay, and all at once everything changed:

> As I stepped into the tiny flat on the fifth floor of a crowded Bombay apartment house, I met him face to face about to begin his morning puja [religious ceremony]. In that moment we both knew the time had come for me to "take interest" in Manipuri dance and its greatest exponent.[6]

Dance historian and theorist Uttara Asha Coorlawala has argued that such an open appeal on the part of Indian artists signifies a hunger for "international exposure" and a desire to achieve "dignity" or a sense of cultural identity for India—"a battered nation emerging from centuries of economic and cultural exploitation."[7] International acclaim has often improved the reception of many Indian dancers at home as well. Coorlawala asserts that, even today, dancers who are celebrated abroad and gain international exposure often "return to a new level of acceptance and respect for their art within India," as their dance, which has been approved by critics and audiences abroad, is now "perceived as epitomizing the highest values of Indian culture."[8]

Priyagopal, then 37 years old, was a distinguished member of the first family of Manipur. He was educated at Calcutta University and apart from being a peerless *Jagoi* dancer, he was also a great archer, polo player and horse rider (Figure 4.1). After completing his initial training under his father, Priyagopal learnt various *Meitei* dances at Kamal Palace in Manipur, under the guidance of a string of legendary gurus. It is said that when Tagore saw a *Jagoi* performance, titled *Vasant Nritya* (Spring Dance), by Priyagopal, he was moved to tears.[9] He was so entranced by Manipuri dancing that he requested Maharaja Surjaboro Singh to start a dance course in Manipuri *Jagoi* at Santiniketan along with other gurus whom Tagore had invited. Priyagopal, following his father's footsteps, joined the art and dance departments of Tagore's famed educational institution. In 1937,

Figure 4.1 Rajkumar Priyagopal Singh, wearing traditional Manipuri attire, photographed with folded hands in *Khamba* dance, 1951.

Source: Photographer: Steele.

Photograph from the Louise Lightfoot Bequest, Monash University.

Photograph Courtesy: Music Archives of Monash University and Mary Louise Lightfoot.

Surjaboro and Priyagopal joined Nritya Kalalaya, an institute opened by Somendra Nath Tagore and Shrimati Tagore, where they trained students in Manipuri dance, particularly *Khamba* and *Ras Lila*.[10]

While teaching and performing in various institutions, Priyagopal felt that as a more modern (western) style of Manipuri dance, performed and enjoyed mainly by girls and children, was becoming popular; the pure and classical form would soon "go out of fashion" and this beautiful "art may be lost" forever.[11] Priyagopal "bought some buildings in a beautiful place near Imphal in the hopes of establishing a training centre for dancers"—the Manipuri Dance Academy.[12] In this new endeavour, his associate Laishram Lakshman Singh, a master percussionist who could play Manipuri *Pung, Khol, Pakhewaj, Dholak, Khanjuri* and *Dafat*, assisted him. In an unpublished memoir, Lakshman Singh notes that in 1941 they performed for Nritya Kalalaya at the New Empire Hall.[13] Priya Gopal performed three items, which included *Mahadeva* dance, *Khamba* dance and *Pala Cholom*. Lakshman Singh performed *Naad Mala* (playing nine *Tablas*) and Anganao (playing of two *Khanjuris*). In 1942, Nritya Kalalaya sent the duo to teach Manipuri dance at Bharatiya Vidya

Bhavan, Bombay (Mumbai). Here, they trained students to perform *Kansa Bhada* (the killing of Kansa) and play Manipuri *Mridangam*.[14] Lakshman Singh remembers that during this period, they also performed to acclaim at Regal Hall. From Bombay, the duo moved to Ahmedabad but ill health brought Priyagopal back to Calcutta and Imphal. In 1944, the Japanese air attack on Imphal brought him back to Bombay.[15]

Priyagopal, who had performed in major dance centres of India, Delhi, Calcutta and Bombay, was more eager to establish himself as a Guru in international dance and was in search of an impresario who had worked with Indian artists abroad. In a letter dated 2 July 1945, Priyagopal requested Louise to publicize his work while promoting Shivaram's performance as a Publicity Director: "Now as you become publicity director you may also publish some writing for me (sic)."[16] In another letter dated 29 June 1946, Priyagopal wrote to Louise: "I am also trying to start one party for India tour and I call you to join me. Let me know whether you have a mind to come here. Will you write to me with all the details ...."[17] As Louise was busy with Shivaram's tour, she was not able to respond. In a letter dated 6 August 1950, Louise wrote to Priyagopal:

> Meanwhile, I am busy on my book of adventures again, trying to finish it up. I have about 50 illustrations but I am sorry I have none of you and I always admired your dancing and your father's teaching. Please send me (if possible by airmail) a photo. It is useless my sending you a money-order to arrange this as you did not answer my last letter and I am not sure where you are.
>
> I often wonder would you be available for a tour abroad and whether you are still dancing and in good form. I have been showing Kathakali style for a long time now but I have a great wish to show Manipuri style, especially with the Manipuri drum. How do you feel about touring? I suppose it would not be easy to leave your wife and daughter. Let me know about the possibility so that I can keep it in mind for future plans. Australia would like to see a new kind of Indian dance. So please write to me soon.[18]

Priyagopal, who was once again employed at Bhartiya Vidya Bhawan and giving private tuitions to wealthy students at Seth Raichand Shah's music and dance academy in Mumbai, enthusiastically replied in a letter dated 31 August 1950:

> I will help you as much as I can regarding the book that you are writing. I will also send you the photos (sic). I am conducting classes

at the above address [Bhartiya Vidya Bhawan, Bombay], which is one of the famous institutions in India.

I am now going to present one big dance ballet ... in November at "Liberty." We are also making a plan to tour all over India and afterwards to Western countries. So I am busy with this work. If you are not bound up there, I would like to invite you to join our Artists Union, in India and abroad.

I am free of family and prepared to go anywhere. I left Shrimati since [sic] one year. I am anxious to hear more about you.[19]

In fact, Priyagopal had left his wife (Shrimati) a year ago and after hearing from Louise became even more impatient to establish his reputation outside India as early as possible.

Seth Raichand Shah deplored in a letter to Priyagopal that he left Mumbai without informing anyone or paying his hotel bills. He alleged that this was an unfortunate incident as Priyagopal also took all the costly instruments and costumes of the dance institute with him. Seth Raichand Shah, worried about the sudden disappearance of his star dancer and tutor, even offered monetary help and an assurance to organize shows for Priyagopal whom he considered a cultural ambassador of Manipuri culture. He wrote:

You left Bombay without informing me. I am sorry to know it. Now what about our classes in Bombay. What shall I tell them, what face can I show to all my relatives.

You have also taken all our costumes and musical instruments with you. Please let me know immediately now what is your plan. What will you do with them. When will you come to Bombay again. What shall I do here. May I come to Manipur. If my help is necessary there, will you bring whole party by giving shows at different places. May I send money for you to give shows if necessary. You have made my position very bad here. I cannot show my face to anyone. What people will say when they will hear about you. When you are a good artists you can do a lot for your culture. Please answer me by the next post. Make me clear what I have to do. Here all students are asking for our classes. What may I answer them. It would have been better if you would have been contacted me before going. Any way you let me know what is to be done now. What about our all goods. Mr Dixit was asking for your hotel bills of 135 Rs. May I pay him. Have you dispersed our goods in Bombay or have you taken all goods with you. Please let me know all things about our costumes and instruments. I am anxious to know *(sic)*.[20]

As may be well imagined, Priyagopal never replied to Seth Raichand Shah.

With Priyagopal as her guide, Louise travelled to the remote mountain state of Manipur to learn more about other forms of Hindu dances. She writes:

I found myself airily crossing Bengals' great serpentine rivers, the Ganges and the Brahmaputra, and effortlessly climbing above range after range of mountains, finally to skim round the rim of a perfectly level plain and so descend into the secret land, so like *mani* (a jewel), ringed by many ranges of mountains! No wonder that the sages of old thought it to be the navel of the world![21]

In Imphal, Louise stayed in an old British army building. This place was being used as an office for a local contractor, Yumnam Gourmani Singh. This contractor and builder were awarded the project of constructing the academic building of D. M. College.[22] Louise started recording her own observations of Manipur and Manipuri dance and continued to read about the history and practice of various dance forms including *Jagoi* (a rhythmical and dramatic dance performed with drums and cymbals).[23] Louise notes:

Many fine books have been written about the Dances of India both by Indians and Westerners; but invariably the chapters or paragraphs about Manipur have been both inadequate and incorrect. Without waiting for research-subsidy from any Government or Society, I decided to stay at least a couple of years in Manipur and write what I considered more suitable information about the background of Manipuri Dancing—or rather "Meitei Jagoi" as I prefer to call it.[24]

She wrote in her 1958 book, *Dance-Rituals of Manipur, India: An Introduction to "Meitei Jagoi"*:

Although my stay in Manipur was a most happy one, it was not without a few difficulties. The Meiteis of Manipur are distrustful of foreigners, and indeed for good reasons! Their fertile valley has been coveted many times and they have struggled hard to keep possession of it. There is a game among the children there called "Kwak Mayang" in which they cling behind each other in line while their leader swerves about protecting them from the attack of the Kwak Mayang (Foreign Crow). There were many times when I was made to feel like a Kwak Mayang. Little boys jeered at me on the road as though I were an outcast. One even spat. Older youths encouraged them by laughing while men condoned this sport in silence. Occasionally older men reproved *(sic)* them, and I remember once a little chap received a severe smacking for mocking me while I stood watching a Lai Harouba [Lai Haraoba] ritual. Once, when passing by a group of young men on the road, the Meitei friend who was accompanying me overheard unsuitable remarks. He continued to walk on a little distance and then decided to go back and explain about my visit instead of scolding them. The group welcomed this idea.[25]

Though Louise "suffered attacks of loneliness in Manipur" along with other problems—some that stemmed from the initial mistrust of Manipuri people—and some logistical ones, such as no taxis or hire cars, and difficulty in communication and no proper interpreter. She overcame these difficulties with good nature and through an ability to make friends with locals everywhere.

Yet I was patient and the knowledge I gained was perhaps not so extensive but the Meiteis opened their hearts to me. They were not content till I had danced before the shrines of their ancestors in their own dress at the Lai Harouba (an unheard of event for a European, as far as I know) and boys along the road greeted me with the request not to wear European dress any more. Neighbours' little ones stopped crying at the sight of a woman "too white" and became pals with me at last.[26]

Louise passionately studied Manipuri dance and culture, much to the surprise of both Priyagopal and Y. Gourmani Singh. Louise wrote:

It was amazing how at first he [Y. Gourmani Singh] was not able to imagine that I could be really interested in ancient Meitei culture. When, in my enthusiasm, I one evening ordered my own rickshaw, he was shocked. When I purchased my own cycle he could scarcely hide his displeasure. On learning I was cycling off to a Lai Harouba (festival-dance) one afternoon, he offered his car; but on arriving at the grounds he refused to enter them with me and sat outside waiting. But so persistent and enthusiastic was I that by the end of my stay he had become a competent convert to his own Meitei culture and especially to the Lai Harouba.[27]

Priyagopal also introduced Louise to Lakshman Singh and S. Kulla Singh. Louise had finally found the artists for her next adventure. Before their Australian tour, in 1949, Louise led the three Manipuri dancers as impresario to perform in the All India Cultural Conference at Delhi. This performance was lauded in national newspapers.

Finally in 1951, Lightfoot as the Stage Manager and Artistic Director of Priyagopal and Lakshman started making all the necessary arrangements and getting together paperwork for the first Manipuri dancers to tour Australia.[28] Mary Louise Lightfoot observes that this time, both the Indian and Australian immigration officials were kind to Louise's cause:

> There were reams of paperwork to make her plans possible and many telegrams backward and forward to Australia ... Louise had to lodge financial securities with both the Indian Congress government for their exit, and with the Australian Immigration authorities for their entry ... These securities were to ensure that the artists would return or be sent back safely to their own country.[29]

Another major concern for Louise was to figure out a way to present Manipuri dances on stage. Manipuri dances were usually performed in large groups as communal dance rituals and original dance compositions were too lengthy for a modern concert programme. Louise, with the help of the artistes, condensed the dances and designed some modern presentations with costumes, ornaments and recordings of music for the Australian stage, without uprooting the original Meitei tradition and its spiritual connotations. It must have been a rare cultural insight for both the Australian audiences and the Manipuri performers to witness and present shortened Manipuri dances on stage.

The trio boarded the ship *Stratheden* and reached the port of Freemantle on 4 July 1951. Both Priyagopal and Lakshman were travelling out of India for the first time. Lakshman, who was to be Priyagopal's *vadya visharad* (Master Drummer or Master of Rhythm) for the Australian tour, carried seventeen different types of hand drums (including other percussion instruments: *mridangam, tabla, dholak, pakwaj* and *caur*) with him, for the performance for a repertoire of forty dances that Priyagopal prepared in consultation with Lightfoot.[30] Most newspapers reported on Lakshman's forte in handling three or more drums at the same time and also on his dance, performed superbly while playing the drums (Figure 4.2).[31]

Figure 4.2 (Left to Right) Lakshman Singh, playing a traditional Indian drum, and Rajkumar Priyagopal Singh, dancing dressed as Krishna, photographed in a dance sequence, 1951.

Source: Photographer: Steele.

Photograph from the Louise Lightfoot Bequest, Monash University.

Photograph Courtesy: Music Archives of Monash University and Mary Louise Lightfoot.

Priyagopal, who was also a cousin of the Maharaja of Manipur, did not use the title of "Prince" as a prefix during his tour, as he wanted to travel like any other Indian artist.[32] However, as the news of his royal lineage spread through newspapers, as part of Lightfoot's marketing strategy to bring in more audiences, journalists lined up to see the Indian dancing prince.[33] Priyagopal was also considered by many in the Australian media and popular opinion as the successor of the now legendary and unforgettable Shivaram, whose personality and recitals many Australians remembered fondly. Melbourne, which was still recovering from the charm of Shivaram's dancing, found in Priyagopal and his form of Manipuri dance a worthy rival. *The Age* (20 August 1951) observed:

Priyagopal danced at the Ballet Guild, 470 Bourke Street, on Saturday evening, and created a strong impression by his vigorous rhythms in a dynamic style that should command more popular appeal than that of the poetic and profound Shivaram.[34]

A letter dated 11 July 1951 to the Editor of *The West Australian*, by Terpsichore, a theatre enthusiast and regular contributor, points not only to the rising popularity of Indian dance styles but also the escalating prices of the ticket for these shows. Terpsichore wrote:

> I am sure that there are many persons like myself who would very much like to see the Indian dancers who are giving performances at the Patch Theatre next week. Because there is only one price, namely 10/, many of us cannot possibly afford to go. Surely the Adult Education Board could have some cheaper seats, so that a greater section of the public could enjoy this educational and unusually skilful form of entertainment. About three years ago we were much more fortunate and were able to enjoy seeing this *very* beautiful Indian Temple dancing by Shivaram at extremely moderate prices.[35]

Fred Alexander, Director of Adult Education Board, and the man who introduced Shivaram to Western Australia, in his reply to Terpsichore through the Editor of *The West Australian* (12 July 1951) wrote back:

> The Adult Education Board shares the regret of your correspondent "Terpsichore" that it is not possible to adhere to its usual policy of providing a substantial number of seats at low prices for the current season of Indian dancers (Priyagopal and Lakshman). Patch Theatre—the one hall available—has 120 seats, each ensuring the same intimate view of the stage. The price charged (10/) is two-thirds that paid by many thousands for the recent National ballet season in Perth. It is the minimum considered necessary to cover presentation costs, living expenses of the artists and their manager while in Perth and their rail transport to Melbourne, instead of through passage by ship, and to make some small contribution towards the over-head expenses in equipment and travel from the remoteness of Manipur.

The board's alternative was to let the dancers bypass Perth and so deny those West Australians with a special interest in this unusually high-quality Indian dancing an opportunity to see worthy successors of Shivaram. If the response to the current season is sufficiently encouraging, the board plans to present the Indian dancers to larger audiences at its customary varied prices, in the Somerville Auditorium, if they return to India via Perth in the summer of 1953.[36]

The Board was eventually successful in sponsoring the two doyens of traditional Manipuri dances, Priyagopal and Lakshman, to the Western

Australian audiences. With the support of the Adult Education Board and the Arts Council of Australia, Priyagopal and Lakshman eventually presented some notable and scintillating performances at:

- Patch Theatre (Perth, July 1951);
- Winthrop Hall, the University of Western Australia (Perth, October 1951);
- Australia Hall (Adelaide, August 1951);
- Ballet Guild (Melbourne, August–September 1951);
- GAMA Theatre (Geelong, September 1951);
- Independent Theatre (Sydney, September 1951); and
- Somerville Auditorium, the University of Western Australia (Perth, January 1952).

During their twelve months tour (from July 1951 to June 1952) of Australia and New Zealand, they performed across their forty-dance repertoire, including *Unganad* (a dance with tambourine), *Nata-Bhangi* (a cymbal and drum dance characterized by agility), *Nada-Mala* (a dance with cymbals and nine drums), *Shiva Sanghar* (a dance showing Shiva as Great Destroyer, Creator and Preserver), *Undro Meipham* (a fire dance), *Khau Sarol* (a spear dance) and *Sagol Bad* (a dance-drama from the *Mahabharata*). The highlight of this tour must surely have been *Khamba-Thoibi* (a dance based in ancient folklore) and *Vasanta Nritya* or *Vasanta Rasa* (a Spring Dance).[37] *Khamba-Thoibi* is a duet dance dedicated to the sylvan deity Thangjing of Moiran and often performed as a part of Lai Harouba [Lai Haraoba]. It typically re-presents the *Tandava* and *Lasya* aspects of Lai Harouba movements by telling the story of Khamba, a poor but brave lad of the Khumal clan who fell in love with Thoibi, a princess of Moirang. Their union was resisted by Moirang chiefs and the result was a tragic one for both the young lovers and the feuding tribes of Manipur. *Khamba-Thoibi* begins with slow movements of the hands and slow beating of the feet on the ground and gradually the tempo rises, the performance ending with a *namaskar* (bow) to the gods and spectators. *Vasanta Nritya* is scheduled in spring when Holi, the festival of colours, is celebrated by the Hindus. This dance is usually performed on *Purnima* (the full moon), takes four hours to complete and is invariably preceded by the *Natapala*, the group of men dancers who play the drum and sing. By setting the tone and mood, the singers and dancers take the audiences into the world of Lord Krishna, Chandravali and Radha in Vrindavan where the *gopis* are playing Holi with them. The dance has its origin in *Brahma Vaivarta Purana*, *Padma Purana* and *Geet Govindam*.[38]

Before their Australian tour, both Priyagopal and Lakshman were well-known in India. This was, as noted earlier, their first trip abroad and that too in front of an audience unacquainted with either Manipur or its culture.[39] *Jagoi* was a form of dance rarely seen or even heard of by Australians—and it did not look "Indian" at all: dancers were dressed differently, did not wear ankle-bells or slap their feet forcefully on the floor as Kathakali, Bharatanatyam and Kathak dancers did. Shivaram's tour and recitals had already alerted the local Australian dance enthusiasts and journalists to "Hindu dance." Yet—or perhaps in consequence—the duo were appreciated roundly (if in terms that present now as exoticization).

Pat Pearce, of *The Herald* (7 December 1953), felt that Priyagopal and Lakshman's recitals and experimentation "proved not only interesting in its own right" but also "a fascinating demonstration of the modification which one dance form can develop."[40] Similarly, John Clifford in *The Australasian Post* (30 August 1951) started his piece with the stereotypical image of Indian tribal dancers and wrote about Priyagopal and Lakshman as if coming straight out "from the wilds of far northern India"—"two small, lithe, brown-skinned men in gorgeous, bespangled dress, with anklets of bells round their legs, and bewildered looks on their faces."[41] But he further observed that "everyone who watched [these two dancers] was immediately captivated [by] the wild beauty of a dance-story that was older than Christendom."[42] Clifford also commended Lightfoot for the work she was doing and noted:

> By then everyone who had seen the dance realised why Louise Lightfoot forsook Australia, and a career in Australian ballet, to live for 12 years among the temple dancers of India. Today she can claim a deeper knowledge of the complex mysteries of Hindu religious dancing than any other white woman. And she is devoting her life to the self-imposed task of bringing Indian dance culture to the notice of the Western world... Despite her years of life in India, Louise Lightfoot says she can't speak any Indian. She is more interested in the Indians' feet than their tongue.[43]

He also praised Priyagopal's dedication and dance. Clifford wrote that Priyagopal danced "using every muscle of his arms, legs, and painted face to express the fears, loves, and anger of the ancient Indian gods, Shiva, Brahma, and Vishnu."[44] K. Catherine of *ABC* pointed out in the Women's Section (1951):

> ... the dances are of all kinds, from religious ceremonial dances, to epic dances; full-bodied, vigorous and infinitely graceful, and with

the most expressive miming of form and movement in hand and arm. It makes me realise how little one knows of the beauty and significance of the dance if one only knows western dancing, the ballet and Greek and the free miming dance. I thought as I watched, what a marvellous instrument the body is when it is used like this; how clumsy we habitually are, immobile, inexpressive, and how good it would be for children all to learn something of these movements. They would not need to grow up holding their torsos and arms like loads of stiff putty.[45]

The *Sydney Morning Herald* (17 September 1951):

Priyagopal's dancing is fluid and graceful—quite sinuous at times—with few of the stiff and formal movements one is inclined to associate with a religious dance.

It can be appreciated without reference to ritual or tradition beyond a general understanding of the legends upon which the dance-dramas are based, for it makes a subtle and beautiful pattern of movement and its miming is at least as specific and intelligible as that of the "expressive" dance of the West.

His art illustrates perfectly the practical value of economy in widening the range of expression, for it develops from a level movement of such intense and hypnotic stillness that the slightest movement of a finger can carry significance and a mere quickening of rhythm can create tension.[46]

Australian audiences seemed to gain new insight into movement and performance art from the Manipuri performances: "caught at times by traditional costuming and the basic elements of all dancing—fluid chor-eographic pattern and the grace, rhythm and expressive line of a dancer himself."[47] Yet the peculiar tension between the viewership and reception of this "exotic" dance form and its proponents' need or expectation of recognition as artists on this international stage persisted and grew. Lightfoot was unable to mitigate what was being lost in translation.

Priyagopal assumed that with all this media attention and reviews in Australian newspapers, he would also get the same audience as his peers, Uday Shankar, Ram Gopal and Shivaram, whose careers were made in the West. However, he ended up doing most of his shows at Australian schools, university clubs and restaurants for very small audiences. On realizing that Manipuri dance would never arrive at the dignity mainland

Indian dances did in Australia, he openly shared his aversion to perform for "mid-afternoon snackers" at a dining hall of an Adelaide department store.[48] In his interview with Clifford, Priyagopal observed:

> It's all so very strange to us here. We are men of religion, and all our dances have religious significance. In India, we dance at temples, or in big homes during religious functions. And the people who come to see us understand our dances. But here no one is of our religion and they do not understand our work. It is very strange to us when we danced in the dining hall the other day. People were sitting round eating and drinking, and waitresses were looking at us from the kitchen door and outside cars were going back and forth. No one was praying, and no one understood. It was very strange.[49]

During the same interview, Lightfoot noted that both he and Lakshman were "still unaccustomed to their strange surroundings" but she hoped they would "get used to dancing before white audiences" and on different platforms soon.[50] The main problem according to Lightfoot was that Priyagopal belonged to the royal family and was not used to seeing such sparse audiences in such frugal settings. Therefore Lightfoot's role and duties as a supervisor (like those of a matron) became more important: "I have to watch over them like a mother—and sometimes bully them a little, too. If it weren't for a bit of ragging from me they would never be on time for their performances or for Press conferences, and photographers."[51]

In contrast with their response to Shankar and Shivaram's dancing, Australian dance journalists, critics and enthusiasts appreciated Priyagopal and Lakshman's "pure and simple" Hindu dancing "free of commercialism" and heavily mediated through Lightfoot's translations and adaptations.[52] Joan L. Erdman has argued that Shankar, as an "authentic" Indian, achieved success and a fine balance between the translation of Indian narratives and recognizable Western language of dance through the use of modern techniques—"an eastern performance" made accessible to western audiences in a "calculated and strategically determined" way.[53] The Manipuri Priyagopal, culturally enmeshed in a crisis of national identity, was not able to bypass Louise's authorship of either his representation as an artist, or of his art. Shankar, with his experimentation with Kathak, Bharatanatyam and Odissi, recognizably Indian dance forms in West, had transcended "Indian dance" genre to a "double global/local identity" as "South Asian dance" genres.[54] Avanthi Meduri has argued that by then Bharatanatyam was not just India's national dance but a South Asian dance par-excellence "dislodged" from India's "sociohistorical moorings."[55]

The very act of translation by Louise that gave prominence to the Manipuri artistes also "marginalised" the dance form to its Australian viewership by designating it as that which "requires explication."[56] The Australian public was obliged to look at Priyagopal and Lakshman's performances through an Orientalist gaze with dancers occupying the position of an "object" rather than the "subject" of knowledge.

Beatrice Ternan, who had seen Priyagopal and Lakshman perform in India during a Festival of Dancing, was bitterly disappointed with the number of people who attended the concert in Australia Hall, Adelaide. In India, she was spellbound by the dancers' artistry and skill. In Australia, the audiences at universities are largely comprised of Indian and Malayan students, dance teachers, ballet-followers, artists, and UN supporters.[57] Ternan, through her letter to the Editor of *The Advertiser* (15 August 1951), pleaded with the public:

> Sir—Instead of playing to capacity audiences in India, Priyagopal, the famous dancer, was persuaded to come to Australia on a cultural tour, being assured that there would be sufficient number of people in each state to support this gesture of sharing with us the rare art the traditional Manipur dance dramas.

As well as being a fine artist, Priyagopal is imbued with an international spirit and maintains that the rhythm of the dance is a universal language that is helping to eliminate national barriers. I saw him in India during a Festival of Dancing and was spellbound by this young dancer's artistry and the scintillating skill of his drummer, and was delighted that Adelaide was to have the good fortune of seeing these artists.

The attendance at Australia on Monday night was bitterly disappointing and in contrast to crowded audiences in Perth and Kalgoorlie. With his equally famous drummer, Priyagopal presented an absorbing and fascinating programme, with such outstanding items as "The Dance of Shiva," "Sacrificial Fire Dance" and the impressive "Spear Drama." There is only tonight and tomorrow night to see these dancers.[58]

Referring directly to Shivaram's trouble in Adelaide, who was refused accommodation because of his nationality and colour, Ternan implored the South Australian public: "Is Adelaide going, once again, to wake up when it is too late?"[59] Similarly, C. B. De Boehme critiquing the dance performance of Priyagopal and Lakshman in Adelaide (13 August 1951) wrote that the two "at times danced as men obsessed."[60] He too urged everyone interested in Indian dance "to attend one of the remaining recitals"—even if only as an entertainment (Figure 4.3).[61]

Figure 4.3 Rajkumar Priyagopal Singh, dressed in a traditional Indian warrior attire, photographed in archer pose, 1951.

Source: Photographer: Steele.

Photograph from the Louise Lightfoot Bequest, Monash University.

Photograph Courtesy: Music Archives of Monash University and Mary Louise Lightfoot

The small Australian audiences were consistently satisfied with what they saw and "for two and a half hours the dancer and the drummer held complete dominion over the audiences."[62] The *Bulletin* observed that in Manipuri dances: "Everything was merged into a continuous rhythmic movement which was as incomprehensible to a person ignorant of the language as it was alluring to the senses."[63] Ultimately, "drawing large enthusiasm from small audiences"[64] for a dance form and culture that was little known within India because of "its inaccessibility" seemed to be facilitating a loyal cult following, for Manipuri dance, and for a "foreign," international dance form as subcultural.[65] An Australian journalist commented:

> I do not think our European civilisation can show anything to equal this; neither the poetry of Shakespeare nor the music of Beethoven can match it. To me it was an ultimate justification of the pain and martyrdom of human life on earth, even though it may, in fact, be the oldest and the most primitive of the arts.[66]

Most of the audiences, who had no idea where Manipur was located in India, felt fortunate to have seen "a new and inspiring vision of the beauty, the dignity, and the power of human expression" and "left the theatre knowing that I had shared in an experience that will remain with me for the rest of my life."[67] Priyagopal, as the main dancer, gathered some rave reviews for his performances as he:

> showed the body control and precise agility of a top-notch athlete, to which was added a technique of wondrous rhythms and colors. There was, too, a devout intentness, great felicity and force of movement, swift changes of tempo and design, and the most subtle use of hands and arms in the dancing.[68]

Lakshman, who appeared primarily as a drummer, also showcased "an amazing exhibition" of drumming that ranged from "the highly frenzied to the exquisitely sensitive" that Australians had never seen before.[69]

Indian critics, like Manorama Kathju of *The Sunday Standard* (2 September 1951), were almost repressively lukewarm. Although Indian audiences had "heard these names fairly often" she wrote, they would not "recall them with pleasant memories" as "their efforts at producing dance dramas proved futile" in Mumbai.[70] Of their dance itself she could say nothing: "the Manipuri dance technique, or for that matter, any Indian dancing—is still unusual fare for Australian audiences, so I reckon their performances will go down well."[71] As Manipuri dance is different in appearance and presentation from forms granted more political legitimacy in India, that Priyagopal and Lakshman were able to impact on Australian audiences at all was considered an achievement in itself. For critics like Kathju, Manipuri dance was India's "non-Indian" style with more folk elements, so the reason for its mark on Australian audiences it must have been visceral and physical, not intellectual and aesthetic:

> Perhaps more than the dancing it is the drumming that has created a sensation and the programmes include a number of solo "mridang" [a percussion instrument] recitals by Lakshman Singh. The drum is considered the king of instruments and plays a very significance [sic] role not only in Indian dancing but in terpsichorean art of Ceylon and of other countries which show Indian influence.[72]

An analysis published by Manipuri dance and literature critic E. Nilkanta Singh in *Marg* (1961), reads like an incredible exercise in political wish-fulfilment through means of art criticism. Priyagopal is characterized at once as the ideal scion, exponent of tradition, and the innovative progressive who may be hoped will transcend his roots:

> [A] worthy son of a worthy father ... most widely travelled artist of Manipur. He is traditional in the sense that his creative compositions like *Shiva-Samhar* betray more of earlier *Laiharaoba* dance technique than of *Ras* tradition and emphasis [sic] the subdued aspect of Manipuri style. His dance movements are characterised by stillness and dignity of restraint. He often breaks conventions and recreates Manipuri dance technique in his own artistic way.[73]

At the end of their Australian and New Zealand tour, Priyagopal, Lakshman and Louise wanted to showcase the Manipuri dance in other countries. The trio decided Japan as their next stop and sailed on *Changte* from Sydney to port Kobe in April 1952.[74] Here, Priyagopal and Lakshman had a fight. Lakshman who felt mistreated at the hands of Priyagopal requested Louise to book his passage back home.

Soon Priyagopal found a wealthy Indian businessman interested in promoting Manipuri dance in Japan. He patched up with Lakshman and asked him to support his big plans for the duo. Unexpectedly for Louise, Priyagopal wanted to cut all ties with her. He believed Louise was the reason behind the rift between the dancer and his drummer. In a letter to her sister Maisie, Louise wrote: "He wanted to teach me a lesson that he could do without me, that I could just help him instead of taking the reins ... He took the show out of my hands."[75]

Letters between Priyagopal and Louise highlight the differences that must have started developing during their Australian tour. Priyagopal took control and Louise felt abandoned:

> When I was left stranded in Japan, Priyagopal refused to give me even one rupee toward my food expenses. My mental and physical health was [sic] both much affected. The Australian Mission was supportive and after several weeks I was able to convince the Australian Government of my serious condition and get some money sent to Japan for living expenses.[76]

As all this unfolded, Louise missed Shivaram's support and jovial nature. She immediately cabled and requested him to join her once again in promoting Indian dance abroad—a proposal Shivaram happily accepted.[77]

Notes

1 Parts of this chapter have appeared as "Louise Lightfoot and Rajkumar Priyagopal Singh: The First Manipuri Dance Tour of Australia, 1951" in *South Asian Popular Culture* (2014). Published here with the permission of Taylor and Francis.
2 Lightfoot, *Lightfoot Dancing*, Chapter 29.
3 Ibid., Chapter 14.
4 After Madhavan's dismissal from Kalamandalam, Shivaram was made in-charge of the Kathakali troupe. He told Poet Vallathol that it is a big task and would need Louise's help. See Ibid.
5 Lightfoot, "In Search of Manipur," 1951.
6 Lightfoot, *Lightfoot Dancing*, Chapter 29.
7 Coorlawala, "Ruth St. Denis and India's Dance Renaissance," 148.
8 Ibid. 147–148.
9 Lightfoot, "In Search of Manipur," 1951.
10 Tamphasana Devi, "The Tagore Family and the Manipuri Dance (1920–1960)," 13921.
11 M.L., "Dancer Holds Secrets of Dying Art," 1.
12 Ibid.
13 Tamphasana Devi, "The Tagore Family and the Manipuri Dance (1920–1960)," 13921–13922.
14 Ibid., 13921.
15 Ibid.
16 Singh, "Letter to Louise Lightfoot," 1945.
17 Singh, "Letter to Louise Lightfoot," 1946.
18 Lightfoot, "Letter to Rajkumar Priyagopal Singh," 1950.
19 Singh, "Letter to Louise Lightfoot," 1950.
20 Shah, "Letter to Rajkumar Priyagopal Singh."
21 Ibid.
22 Danisana, "R. K. Priyagopalsana as Cultural Beacon," 2013. Dhanamanjuri College was established in 1946 under the patronage of the late Maharani Dhanamanjuri Devi.
23 Louise Lightfoot had in her collection the following books and articles on Manipur and various Manipuri dances – Grimwood, *My Three Years in Manipur and Escape from the Recent Mutiny,* 1891; Singh, *Bejoy Punchalee,* 1936; Bowers, "Dance and Opera in Manipur," 1953; Singh, *Manipuri Dances,* 1954; *Manipuri Raasas,* 1954; Singh, *The Art of Manipuri Dances,* 1955; Roy, *History of Manipur,* 1958.
24 Lightfoot, *Dance-rituals of Manipur, India,* 1.
25 Ibid.
26 Ibid., 3.
27 Lightfoot, *Lightfoot Dancing*, Chapter 29.
28 Guru Amubi Singh, because of his association with Shankar, was one of the first Manipuri artists to perform outside Manipur, in places like Calcutta, Ahmedabad and Almorah.
29 Lightfoot, *Lightfoot Dancing*, Chapter 29.
30 "The Passing Show," 7; "64 Drums – 1 Player," 1951.
31 Fidelio, "Dancer and Drummer," 1951.
32 In Manipur, no separate classes of dancing communities or people were created along the lines of *devadasis*. Dancers came from all spheres of Manipur's social life.

33 "Title Not Used," *The West Australian*, 5 July 1951.
34 "Dynamic Indian Dancer Here," 1951.
35 Terpsichore, "Indian Dancer," 11.
36 Alexander, "Indian Dancers," 9.
37 On the use of folklore in Manipuri dance, see Ray, "Boundaries Blurred?" 247–267. For a detailed discussion on aesthetic structure of the Manipuri *Ras Lila*, see Sebastian, "Cultural Fusion in a Religious Dance Drama," 242–311.
38 See Lisam, *Encyclopaedia of Manipur*, 797–798.
39 "Dancer from India," 9.
40 Pearce, "Hindu Dance," 1953.
41 Clifford, "Here's a Dance that's Different," 16.
42 Ibid.
43 Ibid.
44 Ibid.
45 Catherine, "Interview with Louise Lightfoot," 1951.
46 M.L., "Excitement in Art of Dancer," 5.
47 T.B., "Dancer & Drummer Portray India's Age-old Arts," 1951.
48 Clifford, "Here's a Dance that's Different," 17.
49 Ibid.
50 Ibid.
51 Ibid.
52 Sutch, "Ancient Dance Form," 1951.
53 Erdman, "Performance as Translation," 68.
54 Meduri, "Labels, Histories, Politics," 2008a.
55 Meduri, "The Transfiguration of Indian/Asian Dance in the United Kingdom," 300.
56 O'Shea, "At Home in the World?" 178.
57 "Varied Crowd Looks at Temple Dancer," 1951.
58 Ternan, "Dance Dramas," 4.
59 Ibid.
60 De Boehme, "Indian Dancers Show Great Artistry," 1951.
61 Ibid.
62 "Two Dancers from Manipur," 15.
63 "Jagoi," 25.
64 M.L., "Dancer Holds Secrets of Dying Art," 11.
65 "Indian Prince to Dance Here," 1951.
66 "Two Dancers from Manipur," 15.
67 Ibid.
68 De Boehme, "Indian Dancers Show Great Artistry," 1951.
69 Ibid.
70 Kathju, "People and What They're Doing," 1951.
71 Ibid.
72 Ibid.
73 Singh, "Contemporary Gurus and Artists," 62.
74 Lightfoot, *Lightfoot Dancing*, Chapter 30.
75 Ibid.
76 Ibid.
77 Ibid., Chapters 30–31.

5   The Goddess of Dancing[1]

Shivaram arrived in Japan in October 1952 and after a series of performances, left with Louise for Canada and the United States of America in
February 1953. They together worked in San Francisco to promote Indian
classical dance. By 1956, after several years of continuous touring, both felt
the need for some rest. They arrived back in Bombay and from here, parted
ways. Shivaram headed for his home in Kerala and Louise went to Imphal
in Manipur. Here, her primary intention was to complete the research for
her book on Manipuri dance. Louise felt that since her last visit in 1951,
things had changed a lot. She shared her views with the editor of a Bengali
newspaper:

> In the forested hills and around Imphal ... in the town centre, and in
> the Residency garden and its island ... Since my visit in 1951, the
> town has become ugly. I think it is important that a landscape garden
> with appreciation of native flora and conditions should be appointed
> quickly to guard the natural beauty of this historic old capital of the
> Meiteis.[2]

In Imphal, Louise was introduced to an outstanding young dancer—
Kshetrimayum Ibetombi Devi by Y. Gourmani Singh who was Louise's
co-host in 1951. Ibetombi was presented as Gourmani's stubborn
niece who loved dancing.[3] Manjusri Chaki-Sircar has argued that the
socioeconomic status of Manipuri women, despite the onslaught of
colonialism, remained robust within the Meitei society, especially in
the cultural sphere of life. Therefore, most traditional performance
rituals in Manipur are carried out by *Maibis* and *gopis*.[4] Ibetombi was
also well-known in Manipur for her performance of the dance of *Ima
Leimaren*, the Great Mother Goddess of the Meiteis, and as an exponent of *Jagoi* and *Maibi* forms—pre-Hindu ritualistic priestess dance
performed by *Meiteis*.[5]

DOI: 10.4324/9781003205203-6

Ibetombi's father was a peon in the Water Revenue Department and wanted his only daughter to gain an education. In an interview with *The Sangai Express,* Ibetombi remembered how her family was ridiculed by people because of her education, in those days:

> People used to ridicule saying he (my father) was trying to ruin the child and that studying books has made us impure. But my father and I persisted. In our *"manga suba"* class, English was introduced and when I used to read aloud A, B, C to memorize them, they would say, "She's learning the language of the Saheb, she's impure." Such was the attitude then.[6]

This public ridicule of the family depressed Ibetombi, and her only ray of hope was her father's positive attitude:

> That would depress me so much at times. But my father was always positive. He used to say, don't pay heed to their words, let your work show. They'll be forced to eat their words when your name is spread across the State. And his words prove true.[7]

Ibetombi started learning *Meitei* dance at age four. When she was twelve years old, she played the role of Brinda, one of the *gopis*, in *Ras Lila*. The impact of Ibetombi's dancing and singing on audiences was so substantial that they started calling her the goddess of Manipuri dancing—"Brinda-sabi" (The one who plays the role of Brinda, the beloved one).[8]

From the age of twelve to nineteen, Ibetombi trained under such masters as Padma Shri Amudon Sharma and Maisnam Amubi Singh.[9] After that, she gradually began to play roles such as Nityainanda, Chandrabali, Radha and Brinda. As Ibetombi was too engrossed in her dancing, she didn't appear for her school examinations: "I studied for '*taruk suba*' but by then I was already very engrossed in my *jagoi* and *esei* and so I didn't give my exams ..."[10] She became the first female dancer to perform the *Meitei Pung Cholom* (*Poong Cholom*) on stage—a drum dance previously performed only by Manipuri men. By the age of nineteen, she had co-founded Ibetombi Dance Centre with the help of her Y. Gourmani Singh, to teach Manipuri dance to children in Imphal.

Ibetombi had performed for Pundit Jawaharlal Nehru, the first Prime Minister of India, and many other important national and international dignitaries. If we look at the evolution of Manipuri dance, we will notice that as a community performance individual artists were never given due importance.[11] But Ibetombi became so popular that people waited for hours to meet her and book her show.

> I was very popular in my heydays, even a few years back too. I would get invites for the whole year in advance. Sometimes when I come home late after a show or the next day, I would find people have spent the night in my outhouse just to wait for me and to give me invites.[12]

In Manipur, her troupe was paid a total of Rupees 700–800. Additionally, she would also receive from the host, about Rupees 50–100 as *dakhina* (offering or tips) as well as some gifts in kind, such clothes.[13] She reminisced:

> We would get around Rs 700–800 in total from the audience which we would divide between ourselves and some amount like Rs 50–100 per person as *dakhina* from the host. Sometimes I would get as much as Rs 500–600 from the audience besides clothes … In our mind, we were singing the praise of God during our performance. If people accept us, then that is our payment.[14]

Despite, the national accolades and her growing reputation as a dancer and teacher in Manipur, and the income from her dance academy, Ibetombi's financial circumstances did not improve much. As a seventh child amongst ten brothers and sisters, she needed more income to sustain her family.

Ibetombi, like Priyagopal Singh, was related to the royal family of Manipur. Her mother was Rajkumari Tamphasana. Louise taught the English language to Ibetombi and her little dancers at the Ibetombi Dance Centre. In return, she learned the Manipuri dance and language. Ibetombi's knowledge of the area and her contacts in the community helped Louise in conducting research into Manipur's religion, history, songs and dances.[15] Louise wrote:

> The knowledge I gained was perhaps not so extensive, but the Meiteis opened their hearts to me. They were not content till I had danced before the shrines of their ancestors in their own dress at the Lai Harouba (an unheard of event for a European, as far as I know), and boys along the road greeted me with the request not to wear European dress any more.[16]

As friendship and mutual respect between Louise and Ibetombi grew, the young dancer "surprised her more orthodox relatives" by openly expressing her ambition to perform abroad—in Australia.[17] So, senior family members and community leaders consequently approached Louise with a request to "select the finest artists and present their culture abroad once more."[18]

Louise, who was suffering from bouts of loneliness and thinking of weather change at this stage, started preparations to take Ibetombi to Australia. But Priyagopal came to know about this impending tour and wrote a very malicious letter in September 1956 to the person helping Louise prepare for the journey. Priyagopal penned:

> She is not the right person to present the Manipuri art to the world. That is why I am not working with her. She spoils the beautiful feeling and life of Manipuri Art and culture and misrepresents such a beautiful art as tribal dance, music and drums (wild, primitive and uncultured) and Manipuris as tribal people. She introduces this finest art in the world to the audience right from the stage, as mentioned above. I am sick to hear these speeches by her. I am not happy to work with her. I felt so happy and light when I escaped from her hand as if I am relieved from jail. Really, I was imprisoned by her. I take her as the greatest enemy of Manipuri Art and the whole of Manipuri Nation and her people.[19]

In addition to this, Priyagopal also wrote that he was now happily touring with an American—Sunya Shurman.[20] This letter ended up in Louise's file which means the receiver showed no interest in Priyagopal's tirade and trusted Louise completely with Manipuri artists.

In 1956, some problems with the shipping via Suiez Canal delayed the tour by eight months. Eventually, in January 1957, Louise travelled to Calcutta with Ibetombi to obtain the necessary paperwork from the Protector of Emigrants. Louise initially made a request to Australian Immigration authorities for four dancers Ibetombi, Shivaram, Angousingh Chingambam (drummer) and Gulapising Khangembam (singer) to accompany her on this tour. The Immigration Authority approved a six-month tourist visa for the four artists, but Louise could afford the security deposit of Rupees 3,000 for only Shivaram and Ibetombi and was therefore unable to bring Angousingh and Gulapising to Australia. Louise and Ibetombi flew to Perth where Shivaram joined them. Ibetombi had to combine the roles of singer, dancer and drummer for the Manipuri items in the repertory.[21] In 2010, remembering her visit to Australia, Ibetombi told Mary Louise Lightfoot:

Travelling to Australia was full of excitement as I was coming out of a very small place. I was eager to know how people would react to the dance form and my performances ... I was so glad and happy in my heart that [Australians] loved my dancing. I was very much encouraged and never felt very homesick because Australian people welcomed me and appreciated me so much. I can never forget those wonderful days.[22]

While Ibetombi looked upon at this tour as a means to improve her financial position, Louise saw it as an opportunity to encourage a deeper appreciation of the formal complexity and variety of Hindu dancing. She was no longer seeking to present Australian audiences with another ancient, mysterious and spiritual Hindu art form.

Louise presented Ibetombi and Shivaram as the "Star Dancers of India" to the keen and delighted Australian public, first in Western Australia and then in the eastern states. Louise made sure that the audiences learned the difference between "primitive tribal dance"—as Priyagopal has accused her of presenting Manipuri dance abroad—and the cultured *Meitei* dance as performed by Manipuri artists like Ibetombi. The performance programme described Ibetombi as:

Manipur's best female dancer. Without doubt she is one of the world's most graceful and musical dancers. Though only twenty years old, she is devoted to her art and almost fanatical about every detail of rhythm, movement and costume. She excels in the classical dances of Krishna and Radha which are the most exacting in style of any Manipuri dances. She also loves the folk dances of the "Nagas," the tribal people of the Manipur hills. Some of her special interests are research into the origin of Manipur dance, and the revival of ancient songs and dances. ... Ibetombi has unusual intelligence, musicality, grace and stamina.[23]

Louise summarized and shared some chief characteristic features of Manipuri Hindu dancing for the audiences thus:

1   The place or stage where dance is performed is held very sacredly.
2   Dances are mostly devotional or ritualistic in nature rather than entertainment pieces. The artistes never look at the audience directly as a mark of his/her surrender to the deity.
3   The dancer's face in Manipuri style is serene, meditative and smooth.

4   The dressing is free from any sexual stimulus (for co-artistes and audiences).
5   The dancers and artistes do not show feelings of lust, greed, anger, envy, hatred and pride.
6   The steps of dancing are complex and the dancer uses the rounded rhythmic movements and expressions on the upper part of the body.

In Australia, with the help of Louise, Ibetombi developed and presented perfection in her dance technique, which proved "a revelation to Western eyes."[24] Her grace and artistry doubled with the spectacular and authentic costuming provided by Louise and deeply captivated the audience. Australian journalists were amazed by Ibetombi's gentle nature, placid charm and controlled emotions that helped in expressing metaphorical use of dance language (Figure 5.1).

From January to November 1957, Ibetombi and Shivaram toured Australia, New Zealand and Indonesia. With modest support from the Arts Council of Australia, Adult Education Board and the National Theatre Movement of Australia, Louise presented this leading female exponent of *Jagoi*, *Maibi* and *Meitei* dance forms. In Australia, the trio toured for six months:

• Perth (February—Albany Town Hall, Festival of Perth and the University of Western Australia);
• Melbourne (March—National Theatre, Moomba Festival and Alexandra Gardens);
• Hobart (April—National Theatre, Hagley Farm School, Devonport Town Hall, St Marys and St Helens);
• Brisbane (May—Albert Hall);
• Sydney (June—National Art Gallery, ANZAC House Auditorium, Lockhart and Teachers College Bathurst); and
• Canberra (July—Albert Hall).

Ibetombi performed several *Jagoi* dances. The most spectacular included: *Krishna Abhisar* (a devotional solo dance expressing love to Lord Krishna), *Arti Katpa* (a religious prayer dance offered in front of Krishna-Radha temple), *Eema Leimaren* (a dance telling the mythical creation of earth), *Lai Kooroomba* (a devotional dance offered in front of the shrine of Thanging narrating sad love story of Thoibee and Khamba), *Lai Loukatba* (an ancient ritual dance-drama offered to the spirit of Great Being who once dwelt in Manipur) and *Hao Jagoi* (a selection of Naga and Kuki tribal dances).

There were two highlights of her performance. In terms of dance items, it was the presentation of *Ras Lila* and *Poong Cholom*. *Ras Lila*

Figure 5.1 Ibetombi Devi performing dressed as Sri Krishna in *Ras Lila*, 1957.

Source: Photographer: Australian News and Information Bureau.
Photograph from the Louise Lightfoot Bequest, Monash University.
Photograph Courtesy: Music Archives of Monash University and Mary Louise Lightfoot

dance captures both the *Rup* (form) dance highlighting Krishna's beautiful appearance and *Bashi Konjon Taba* dance that highlights Radha's search for Lord Krishna which symbolizes soul's quest for the eternal beloved (Figure 5.2). *Poong Cholom* or *Pung Cholom* (also known as the *Mridanga Dance* or *Dhumel*) dance is either performed as an integral part of *Nat sangkirtan* (*Pala Kirtana*) or as a prelude to *Raas Lila*. During this, the dancer plays the *pung* (a hand-beaten drum) while he or she dances using graceful acrobatic movements. The second highlight of this tour was Ibetombi and Shivaram's brilliant performance on 14 May 1957, titled *Chitrangada*, which was broadcast from Melbourne on Australian Broadcasting Corporations' television programme (9.30 pm to 9.50 pm).[25] This dance-drama is based on a story from *Mahabharata* where Arjuna is on his twelve years vow of celibacy and during his wanderings, reaches Manipur. Here, he meets the warrior princess Chitrangada and is astonished by her fighting skills. Both fall in love and Chitangada agrees to marry Arjuna on one condition that he will treat her as an equal.[26]

As opposed to a group dance, audience expectations from a solo dance performance are higher. But as an expert Manipuri dancer, with her artistic perfection and the accompanying rich music, it wouldn't have been difficult for Ibetombi to hold the Australian audiences' throughout

Figure 5.2 (Left to Right) Ananda Shivaram and Ibetombi Devi presenting hands pose from *Ras Lila* for Australian journalists, 1957.

Source: Photograph from the Louise Lightfoot Bequest, Monash University.

Photograph Courtesy: Music Archives of Monash University and Mary Louise Lightfoot.

her solo performances. Australian journalists were amazed by Ibetombi's gentle nature and controlled emotions that characterized her dance language. A newspaper (3 April 1957) reported: "When for half a second she freezes in some pose or other, with her arms and feet this way and her head like a flower on a bent stalk, she instantly recalls the sculpture on the temples built somewhere around 2000 BC."[27]

Geoffrey Hutton, a columnist for *The Age* (April 1957), noted that Ibetombi "performs the simpler dances of her race with unfailing charm and elegance."[28] R.R. writing for *The Sydney Morning Herald* (7 June 1957) was surprised by Ibetombi's performance:

> Shivaram's fame has preceded him but Ibetombi is a surprise. Shivaram represents the ancient Dravidian race, Ibetombi the Mongol. ... Her native music flows through her being. She is restrained, like any good dancer, with a beautiful, impassive face.
>
> She can withdraw, like an exotic flower, with a delicate, lyrical quality of understatement. She can be possessed by turns of a sensuous, fragrance-exuding languor, a barbarous regal quality or an intense tribal savagery.[29]

R.R., in *The Sydney Morning Herald* (13 June 1957), referred to Ibetombi elsewhere as belonging to the "Mongolian" race, observing a certain congruence between her dance and Mongolian art more generally: "a kind of beauty like a tightened bow, that is not natural in an age like this, a savage, cruel, fierce Mongolian beauty...."[30] David K. Cleaver, an admirer of Indian dance art, was highly offended by this gross and racist comparison.[31] Cleaver wrote a strong letter to the Editor of *The Sydney Morning Herald* (13 June 1957) to point out this as a "popular fallacy":

> As to Ibetombi's art being Mongolian, this, too, is inaccurate. There is no such thing as Mongolian art or dance. The Mongolian peoples of Burma and Siam, though borrowing from the north, in their dance and art are far closer to the Caucasian people of India than to, say, the Koreans or Japanese, who are cousins. This is a popular fallacy, that racial origin plays an important role in influencing cultural traits and character, and is a remnant of the pseudo-scientific nineteenth-century theories of race.[32]

The "Mongolian Fringe," according to Olaf Caroe, the foreign secretary of the British-Indian government, extended from India's northwest Himalayas to the hill regions of the northeast frontier. This division based on racial stereotypes has often resulted in a cultural difference, a paradoxical attitude, prejudice and discrimination towards the indigenous and tribal people from northeast India.[33] For her part, Lightfoot made sure that audiences appreciated the cultured Meitei dance performed by young Manipuri artists such as Ibetombi and did not view her art from a racialized perspective. Lightfoot had studied Manipur dance through scholarly books: Mutua Jhulan Singh's *Bejoy Punchalee: History of Manipur, Parts 1 and 2*; Faubion Bowers' "Dance and Opera in Manipur"; Haobam Kulabidhu Singh's *Manipuri Dances, Manipuri Raasas* and *The Art of Manipuri Dances*; and Jyotirmoy Roy's *History of Manipur*.[34] Consequently, she prepared her explanatory notes scrupulously, delineating some of the principal features of Manipuri dancing, including the understanding of the stage as a sacred space; the devotional or ritualistic character of dance; the absence in the work of dancers of any hint of lust, greed, anger, envy, hatred or pride; and the modest dress worn by dancers or the artist to avoid any sexual stimulus audiences.

Louise's support, allowed Ibetombi to develop and present her dance as high art—"a revelation to Western eyes."[35] The grace and artistry of the dancers in combination with spectacular and authentic costumes, made a deep impression on audiences, as reflected in the press (15 February 1957):

> Australian audiences have never before seen Maibi dance. Probably never before have Albany audiences seen dancing which combined exquisite grace with such perfection of technique. Expressive gestures interpreted a story in many of the dances executed. In India quite often people sang the story behind the dancers, said Miss Lightfoot, but even without this on the Western stage little of the traditional character was lost. … It was noticeable that even strangers to Indian dancing understood the meaning behind significant gestures, rhythm and movements of both Ibetombi and Shivaram.[36]

Ibetombi, who was touring almost sixty cities and towns in Australia, experienced some initial feelings of trepidation. In a letter to *The Ngasi* (8 April 1957), a Manipuri national daily paper, she wrote:

> I must say I was slightly nervous the first day I appeared at the University Hall, Perth to dance on record of music. But as I progressed with another performance I found the whole thing easy. The credit goes to Miss Lightfoot who is steering and providing a narration of Metei culture and Manipur Sena Leipak during the performance. This continental tour encourages me to learn dancing

more assiduously on my return home. I owe all my success to my teachers and Sri Govind whose devotee I am.[37]

Acclimatizing to the Australian food and culture, was also a hurdle for Ibetombi. But she got on very well with Louise who was quite supportive of her artists. Ibetombi told Mary Louise Lightfoot:

> I shall ever be indebted to Louise. I learnt so many things from her. She used to teach me English. She tried hard to make me pronounce the word "FISH" and I used to pronounce it "PHIS" (as Manipuri alphabet also doesn't have either "F" or "SH"). Instead of getting mad with my poor pronunciation we used to burst into laughter. It was full of fun and learning. Louise always treated me like a daughter.[38]

As there were no Indian restaurants, so the dancers cooked simple curry and rice for themselves; Shivaram and Ibetombi were pictured in one of the newspaper interviews as: "Sharing their meal of rice, greens, split peas, chillies and curry...."[39] They bathed in oil "to keep their muscles supple for the sinuous, undulating movements of the exotic temple dances." They had to be careful with the coconut oil as it was in short supply—and they were told that "Australian landlords aren't well disposed to people who swamp their bathroom floors with coconut oil."[40]

Ibetombi's initial fears and nervousness regarding the success of the tour were unfounded. E.D.H. reported in the *Courier-Mail* (18 May 1957) that "Two bare-footed Indians, dancing on a bare stage, kept a Brisbane audience enthralled for more than two hours last night."[41] Constance Cummins, observing Ibetombi's performance, felt that the audiences forgot the winter cold and were transported to India by the exotic colours and strange and enchanting music: "Winter cold was forgotten when the ritualistic movements, tinkling ankle-bells, and rich red and gold costumes of two Indian dancers brought on exotic atmosphere to the Albert Hall last night."[42] As more Australian people saw Ibetombi dance, they discovered that the recitals had a strong educational element, encouraging a wider understanding of Indian culture: "... far from being for us alien and difficult, is surprisingly close to Western ways in much of its motive power and mode of expression."[43] An Indian student, named Kamal, studying under the Colombo Plan at the University of Melbourne, remarked that Ibetombi's dances gave a true representation of his country:

> Indian culture, and indeed India herself, cannot be properly understood and appreciated without an adequate acquaintance with

Indian dance, through which the artistic genius of the Indian people has expressed itself in a manner which is as effective as it is rich and varied.[44]

Mary Louise Lightfoot who was about twelve years old at that time also saw Ibetombi's performance in Melbourne:

> I saw one of their performances in a large auditorium when I was twelve. Dad took me to Melbourne to meet Shivaram and Ibetombi. I remember her doe-like eyes, how quiet, gentle and obedient she seemed to me. I admired her long thick plaits of dark hair, while I hated the thin mousy plaits my mother insisted wear. I remember too the layers of skirts in her dance costumes, like the dresses of some of Louise's Manipuri dolls.[45]

Ibetombi's vivid, graceful movements and her versatility enchanted Australian audiences and created for Indian arts, which had been un-known hitherto, a secure place in the public consciousness, and a basis for the development of further understanding (Figure 5.3).[46] After seeing Ibetombi's dance recitals, R.R suggested that the people of Australia might "realise how much our own ballet could benefit from a study of the beautiful hand and arm movements and the unparalleled restraint of mime."[47] Even in her demonstration of the primitive, tribal Jagoi technique, Ibetombi "revealed most beautifully supple, flowing wrists, hands, and slender arms."[48]

After their Sydney Music Club show at Federation Club, Shivaram got the news that his father was gravely ill. He soon left for Kerala and it was time for Ibetombi to leave as well. Louise and Ibetombi left for Cochin (India) via Indonesia and Singapore, where Ibetombi performed a few dances for the Indian Cultural Society. From Cochin, Louise accompanied Ibeombi to Imphal where she "was welcomed by everyone like a princess."[49]

Ibetombi's Australian tour can be summarized and narrated through the tripartite lens of finance, reputation and cultural understanding. Ibetombi succeeded financially—although she claimed in an interview that money was never a concern for her: "in our mind, we were singing the praise of God during our performance. If people accept us, then that is our payment."[50] Ibetombi earned approximately Rupees 2,800 from her six months Australia tour, an amount far more than her annual earnings in Manipur. Her Australian tour of 1957, in company with Shivaram, established her internationally as an exponent of the *Maibi* and *Jagoi* styles. E. Nilkanata Singh noted that after her tour Ibetombi,

Figure 5.3 Ibetombi Devi, dressed in traditional Manipuri attire, photographed in a dance pose in *Eema Leimaren*, 1957.

Source: Photographer: John Tanner for the Australian News and Information Bureau.

Photograph from the Louise Lightfoot Bequest, Monash University.

Photograph Courtesy: Music Archives of Monash University and Mary Louise Lightfoot.

… emerged as a serious exponent of Manipuri dance and has earned much fame as a remarkable dance artist. Though her mastery of the Ras Dance is beyond doubt, she specialises now in Maibi dance of the laiharaoba style which is gradually receiving increasing recognition as a classical item, more primitive and more traditional. … She is mainly responsible for a return of Maibi dances to stage worthiness and classical heritage.[51]

The news of Ibetombi's success had reached Manipur through the daily newspaper *The Ngasi* (3 May 1957). Tejmani Sharma, a resident of Imphal and an admirer of Ibetombi's dancing, read about the successful Australian tour and sent a letter full of praise to Lightfoot—"friend and guardian of my lovely friend, Miss Ibetombi Devi."[52] She wrote:

I am praying day and night, and heart and soul to the Great-Almighty for your and your companion's greater and brighter success in the proceeding adventures, I am pleased to say, throughout the World. I heartily request you to lead my friend in the right path and help her in times of happiness as well as of adversities in her life, over so above you have made her a woman, in the real sense of the term. *(sic)*[53]

Coorlawala notes that even today, dancers, who are acclaimed abroad and have international exposure, often "return to a new level of acceptance and respect for their art within India" as "dance is perceived as epitomizing the highest values of Indian culture."[54]

During her Australian tour, Ibetombi Devi demonstrated considerable skill and grace in her solo dances and also sang folk songs of Manipur "in a sweet, plaintive voice."[55] With her keen musical sense, she created the impression that her "every attitude was a fragile, frozen pose that seemed to live again in some temple frieze and bas-relief."[56] Australian audiences appreciated that "Western culture holds no monopoly in the arts—Indian dancers, Chinese poets and primitive African sculptors can possess equal, or even greater, gifts of expression."[57] The appeal of Manipuri dancing for the Australians was akin to that of American audiences, residing—according to Christel Stevens—"not in its points of congruence with other Indian dance styles, but in its points of contrast."[58]

Louise spent considerable time in Manipur to finish her research on local dance tradition and culture. Her research findings resulted in a marvellous monograph titled *Dance-rituals of Manipur, India: An Introduction to Meitei Jagoi* and her recording of songs and ritual music was released as *Ritual Music of Manipur.*[59] In 1958, Louise was planning to move on and things turned sour with Ibetombi's uncle. In disagreement, Y. Gourmani Singh sent Louise a bill for accommodation, excursions and his services incurred in both 1951 and 1958. Louise wrote back that she had in fact given more in return through private tuitions, English language teaching at Ibetombi Dance Centre, advice and superintendence work:

> You had always introduced me as your guest. Now I am relegated to paying guest, and since you prefer now to be rent-collector instead of the host, I would be foolish not to adjust my own attitude accordingly. As you did not present any account or accept any payment proposal since her first visit in 1951, I had given return services so as not to be under any obligation. On account of your sudden change of attitude, this service, therefore, cannot be considered free.[60]

Mary Louise Lightfoot believes that Louise never submitted this invoice to Y. Gourmani Singh. With the sudden change of circumstances and disagreement with her local host, Louise left Manipur for Kerala and Ibetombi never saw her again.

Notes

1 Parts of this chapter have appeared as "Louise Lightfoot and Ibetombi Devi: The Second Manipuri Dance Tour of Australia, 1957" in *Dance Research* 32, no. 2 (2014): 208–232. Published here with the permission of Edinburgh University Press.

2 Lightfoot, *Lightfoot Dancing*, Chapter 33.

3 "Artistry of Indian Dancers thrills Devonport Audience," 1957.

4 For a discussion on status on women in Manipuri society, see Chaki-Sircar, *Feminism in a Traditional Society*, 213–214; Sebastian, "Cultural Fusion in a Religious Dance Drama," 79–80.

5 For a detailed discussion, see Brara, *Politics, Society and Cosmology in India's North East*, 136–137.

6 Samom, "Thokchom Ibetombi Devi," 2008.

7 Ibid.

8 Ibid.

9 Amudon Sharma (1886–1976) was an eminent guru of Manipuri dance. He received the Sangeet Natak Akademi award for Manipuri dance from the Government of India in 1961 and the Padma Shri in 1972. Maisnam Amubi Singh (1881–1972), also known as Oja Amubi, was a well-known Manipuri dance Guru. In 1956, he received the Sangeet Natak Akademi award from the Government of India.

10 Samom, "Thokchom Ibetombi Devi," 2008.

11 Also see, Bandopadhay, "Manipuri Dance," 142.

12 Samom, "Thokchom Ibetombi Devi," 2008.

13 "Artistry of Indian Dancers Thrills Devonport Audience," 1957.

14 Samom, "Thokchom Ibetombi Devi" 2008.
15 "Indian Temple Dancer," 32; See also Samom, "Thokchom Ibetombi Devi," 2008.
16 Lightfoot, *Lightfoot Dancing*, Chapter 33.
17 "Ibetombi—Biographical Note," 1957.
18 "Louise Lightfoot—Biographical Note," 1957.
19 Lightfoot, *Lightfoot Dancing*, Chapter 33.
20 Sunya Shurman (1909–1996) was an American dancer who appeared on Broadway in the Ziegfield Follies and also operated Shurman School. See Lille, *Equipoise*, 83.
21 See Lightfoot, "Letter to Protector of Emigrants (Bombay)," 1951.
22 Lightfoot, *Lightfoot Dancing*, Chapter 33.
23 "Ibetombi – Biographical Note," 1957.
24 See "Indian Dance Recital," 2.
25 For this performance they received a fee of AU$30 from ABC. See Lightfoot, *Lightfoot Dancing*, Chapter 33.
26 This dance-drama was created in 1892 by Gurudev Tagore. He adapted the story of Chitrangada from the *Mahabharata* and expanded the narrative with a feminist characterization of a warrior princess. In Chitrangada, Tagore saw feminine attributes and personification of love, courage and substance.
27 "Indian Dancers," 1957.
28 Hutton, "Exotic Indian Dancer," 1957.
29 R.R., "Traditional Dances of India," 1957.
30 R.R., "Recital of Hindu Dances," 1957.
31 Cleaver, "Indian Dancing," 1957.
32 Ibid.
33 In contemporary times, people from northeast have been racially abused with derogatory words such as "Mongolian," "Chinese," "flat-nosed" or "Chinky." For a detailed discussion, see Baruah, "India," 82–86; McDuie-Ra, *Debating Race in Contemporary India*, 1–31; Gergan and Smith, "Theorizing Racialization through India's 'Mongolian Fringe,'" 2021.
34 See Singh, *Bejoy Punchalee*, 1936; Bowers, "Dance and Opera in Manipur," 1953; Singh, *Manipuri Dances*, 1954; Singh, *Manipuri Raasas*, 1954; Singh, *The Art of Manipuri Dances*, 1955; Roy, *History of Manipur*, 1958.
35 "Indian Dance Recital," 2.
36 "Indian Dances Fascinated Albany Audiences," 1957.
37 Devi, "Manipuri Dance Presented Abroad," 1957.
38 Lightfoot, *Lightfoot Dancing*, Chapter 33.
39 "Indian Style for Their Curry, too," 1957.
40 "The Language of Muscles," 1957.
41 E.D.H., "Two Indian Dancers Enthral Audience," 1957.
42 Cummins, "Indian Dancers Give Exotic Performance," 1957.
43 Fidelio, "Indian Pair Show Vivid Dance Art," 1957.
44 Kamal, "Indian Dancing is a Highly Developed Art," 1957.
45 Lightfoot, *Lightfoot Dancing*, Chapter 33.
46 "Dancer Collects Shells," 1.
47 R.R., "Traditional Dances of India," 1957.
48 R.R., "Recital of Hindu Dances," 1957.
49 Lightfoot, *Lightfoot Dancing*, Chapter 33.
50 Samom, "Thokchom Ibetombi Devi" 2008.

51 Singh, "Contemporary Gurus and Artists," 64; See also, Cleaver, "Indian Dancing," 1957.
52 Sharma, "The Goddess of Dancing," 1957.
53 Ibid.
54 Coorlawala, "Ruth St. Denis and India's Dance Renaissance," 147.
55 B.B., "Indian Dancers Artistic," 1957.
56 R.R., "Recital of Hindu Dances," 1957.
57 T.B., "Dancer & Drummer Portray India's Age-old Arts," 1951.
58 Stevens, "Bringing Manipuri Dance to the World Stage," 2006.
59 See Lightfoot, *Dance-rituals of Manipur, India*, 1958; Lightfoot, *Ritual Music of Manipur*, 1960.
60 Lightfoot, *Lightfoot Dancing*, Chapter 33.

Conclusion

Over the years, Manipuri dance productions have been very well received, with many dance critics noting the striking amalgam of traditional continuity and experimentation and innovations taking place in performance. The evolution of Manipuri dances from a folk form to a more ritualistic form has happened because of the Manipur state's cultural assimilation with India and Hinduism. According to Khoni, this can be read positively, as a "synthesis between two cultures—notably what is presented by the Indian classical texts under Hinduism and the performance tradition of the Manipuri under the Meetei religion."[1] To the inexperienced eye, the variances between different *gharanas* (schools) of Manipuri dance practiced by such gurus and disciples of the Bishnupriya Manipuri, Santiniketan, Manipuri Nartanalaya, the Jawaharlal Nehru Manipur Dance Academy and other institutions are hard to comprehend.

Further, the empanelled artistes of the Indian Council for Cultural Relations (ICCR) perform in various prestigious dance festivals and have also represented India as part of official cultural delegations abroad to showcase the originality and uniqueness of Manipuri culture and its traditions.[2] A major factor in the promotion of Manipuri dance, and in the elevation of its status, has undoubtedly been the exposure provided to the local artists in foreign countries and their collaborations with visiting dancers. It remains arguable, however, whether the visibility and popularity of Manipuri dance have accompanied a just appreciation of technique. Practitioner and scholar Sruti Bandopadhay characterizes it thus:

> The technique of Manipuri dancing have *(sic)* fascinated the audience all over the world for their lyrical manifestation of devotion. The hand gestures used in *Laiharaoba* are the seeds of expression of Manipuri dance. The communication of substance is through the position of the fingers placed in space. The hand gestures used are decorative, interpretative, and suggestive. The

DOI: 10.4324/9781003205203-7

movement patterns in space write the basic vocabulary of the dance form. The facial expression is not stressed much. The face bears a subdued, devotional, and eloquent look.[3]

Bimbavati Devi, in an interview commenting on the status of Manipuri dance in India and abroad, notes that it is wrong to perceive it as monotonous, slow and repetitive:

> We have tried to infuse verve and color into the dance form by being inspired by several aspects of Manipuri dance, for example—the movements of *pung cholom* and *kartal cholom*. Their movements are very stylized and dignified. We want to make people aware of the richness of Manipuri dance.... I want people to know that Manipuri dance is not just a dance wearing the big round costume ... we wear that only in traditional *ras leelas*. But *ras leelas* are popular because they are so lively and the dress is so colorful and bright. We are trying to propagate and perpetuate this dance form far and wide.[4]

The process of perpetuating appreciation of the nuances of Manipuri dance has also helped in increasing awareness about Manipur's other vibrant cultural traditions and heritage on the international stage. According to Sunil Kothari, in 1950s India, it was the Jhaveri sisters (Nayana, Ranjana, Suverna and Darshana) who made Manipuri dance "stage-worthy for urban audiences from traditional night long performances, retaining the core of tradition and yet make them accessible to metropolitan audiences."[5] In fact, the Jhaveri sisters also became the first non-Manipuris to perform their dances at the Shree Shree Govindji Temple inside the royal palace of Imphal.[6]

Dancers such as the Jhaveri sisters, Sougaijam Thanil Singh, Suryamukhi Devi, N. Amusana Devi, Akham Lakhmi Devi, Ibemubi Devi, Tondon Devi, Arambam Tombinou Devi, Elam Indira Devi, R. K. Thambalsana Devi, Kalavati Devi, Binodini Devi, Rajkumar Singhajit Singh, Debjani Chaliha, Sanjib Bhattacharya, Urmimala Das, Bimbavati Devi, Sohini Ray, Sruti Bandopadhay, Priti Patel, Poushali Chatterjee, Latasana Devi, Indrani Devi, Manorama Devi and Sinam Basu Singh, have found their calling in Manipuri dance and helped it garner acclaim on the international stage.[7] Their story, journey and contribution in popularizing Manipuri dance on the global stage would make the comprehensive book.

For their contribution to Manipuri dance, R. K. Singhajit Singh and Darshana Javeri have been awarded prestigious awards such as the Padma Shri.[8] However, no such national award has been conferred upon Louise

Lightfoot, Priyagopal Singh and Ibetombi Devi. As early image-makers in both pre- and post-independent India, these three artists de-provincialized and popularized Hindu dances in the international dance circuit. They organized this unique space as a utopian dream for multicultural dance and the arts that paved the way for other Indian classical and folk dancers as well.[9] These notably included Tilakavati, Indrani, Bhaskar, Chitrasena Ballet, Song and Dance Theatre, Kalakshetra, Kerala Kalamandalam, Balagopalam, Masked Dancers of Bengal, V. Gayatri, Krishnaveni Lakshmanan, Yamini Krishnamurti, Vyajayanthimala, Daksha Sheth, Jyotikana Ray, Mallika Sarabhai, Sonal Mansingh, Birju Maharaj, Sanjukta Panigrahi, Bimbavati Devi, Guru Banamali Sinha, Sruti Bandopadhay and many others. Over the years, these artistes have come to participate in various dance and cultural festivals organized throughout Australia.

In 1951, the Indian Government Trade Commissioner's office commended Louise Lightfoot's passion for promoting Indian dance abroad. They noted: "Her ambition and mission in life is cultural revival of India and propagation of this art abroad. She has made untiring efforts to spread this cultural message in Australia and New Zealand."[10] It has been a great challenge for traditional Hindu dancers, especially Manipuri, to experiment with the age-old tradition.[11] Like many modern cross-cultural collaborations, the dancers Louise worked with too were interested in presenting the traditional Hindu dances alongside contemporary choreographies beyond the boundaries of India. Finally, these Australian tours could not have been possible without the official assistance and support of the Adult Education Board and the Arts Council of Australia—public investment in the arts and a broad-based international outlook were crucial.

During the 1960s, some of Louise and Shivaram's main artistic work continued in San Francisco (United States). The duo educated the American public in Indian dance and eventually taught it to hundreds of students. Shivaram settled down in the United States and started a dance school in partnership with Louise to promote Kathakali through lecture demonstrations in American and Canadian universities and galleries. Building on the project that Poet Vallathol started in the 1920s, Shivaram succeeded in promoting Hindu dance at both national and international levels by gaining recognition for himself as a global cultural citizen and for Kathakali as a classical art among "the world's great classical arts."[12]

Similarly, the first international Manipuri dance tour also established Rajkumar Priyagopal's reputation as a "cultural Guru of the State."[13] He joined the ranks of luminaries in Manipur dance such as the most eminent *gurus* of our time Guru Amubi Singh, Guru Thambal Angou

Singh, Guru Chaoba Singh, Guru Haobam Atomba Singh, Guru Amudon Sharma, Guru Thingbaijam Babu Singh, Guru Amusana Devi, Guru Tombi Sharma, Guru Bhaigchandra Singh and Guru Koireng Singh. After touring Australia, New Zealand and Japan, Priyagopal taught Manipuri dance in India. In 1972, he became the Principal of the Jawaharlal Nehru Manipuri Dance Academy in Imphal (Figure 6.1). Established in 1954, this is one of the oldest, leading institutions in India for teaching Manipuri Dance. Today, the institution is a constituent unit of the Sangeet Natak Akademi and is responsible for organizing cultural programmes both inside and outside Manipur. Here, Priyagopal was instrumental in the production of three famous Manipuri historical ballets—*Bhagyachandra*, *Chaitanya Mahaprabhu* and *Nongpok Panthoibi*. His master drummer Lakshman also established his institution of dance—Manipur Sangeet Mahavidyalaya.[14]

While Priyagopal and Lakshman have passed away, Ibetombi Devi is alive. On her return to India, she married a Manipuri dancer and musician Nava Chandra Singh (Figure 6.2). They have two children—a son and a daughter. Ibetombi's youngest daughter is also an accomplished dancer. In 1984, to keep the tradition of Manipur's *Gourangalila* alive, Ibetombi along with like-minded artistes formed the All Manipur Gourangalila and Sansenba Artists' Association.[15] For her contribution to Manipuri dance for popularizing Meitei dance outside Manipur, Ibetombi received the Republic Day Medal of Dance (1964), the State Kala Akademi Award (1992), Nritya Bhushan Sahitya Parishad (1999) and Guru Tarunkumar Shanman (2006). In 1992, she was awarded the prestigious Manipur State Kala Academy award in recognition of her enduring contribution to the understanding of Meitei Jagoi. After serving as a teacher of Manipuri dance for thirty years in Banasthali Vidyapeeth and as visiting guru at Jawaharlal Nehru Manipuri Dance Academy, Ibetombi is leading a retired life in Imphal. From September 2016, she received the "Grant for Art Scheme" for a period of two years with monthly support of Rupees 5000.[16]

Louise lived and worked at the yoga ashram of Swami Vishnudevananda in Montreal, Canada.[17] In 1967, she returned to Melbourne and lived a simple life. Louise never married and finally retired in 1968. Mary Louise Lightfoot notes that Louise wanted to retire in "a cottage with a cat and geraniums, somewhere north of Sydney."[18] Even in retirement, Louise stayed actively involved in multicultural dance performances and festivals especially at Monash University's Department of Music.[19] At Monash, she worked closely with Australia-based Indian dancers, presenting dancers from India and leading the way for multicultural dance traditions and expressions to find a place in the

Figure 6.1 (Left to Right) Rajkumar Priyagopal Singh and Laisram Lakshman Singh, sitting dressed in traditional Indian men's attire, posing for Australian journalists, 1951.

Source: Photograph from the Louise Lightfoot Bequest, Monash University.

Photograph Courtesy: Music Archives of Monash University and Mary Louise Lightfoot.

Figure 6.2 Ibetombi Devi, dressed in traditional Manipuri attire, demonstrating a *mudra* in *Nityaras*.

Source: Photograph: *NCPA Quarterly* 3, no. 3 (September 1974), 31.

https://www.sahapedia.org/ncpa-quarterly-vol-3-no-3-september-1974#lg=1&slide=0.

Photograph Courtesy: National Centre for the Performing Arts, Mumbai

Australian imagination.[20] In July 1976, Guru Banamali Sinha, a leading exponent of Manipuri dance, performed at Monash University. Sinha was head of Manipuri Dance in the College of Hindustani Music, University of Lucknow and introduced his style to Ballet Victoria.[21]

Louise became ill with pneumonia and died on 18 May 1979 at Malvern. She was buried in the Cheltenham cemetery. Louise's sister Lal told Mary Louise Lightfoot:

> Her last years were not very happy ones. She spent a lot of time in the hospital, which did not please her or suit her at all. As fast as she recovered from one thing, another happened. Mais had to keep her contented in Oakleigh after being all around the world. It was very much a narrowing of interests. Though she kept up her interest in music, dancing and singing, she was not able to do much.[22]

The *Indian Express* (2 July 1979) lamented the death of "Kathakali's Australian mother." Louise's life work in Australia was very similar to one of her American contemporaries, Stella Kramrisch. In 1982, the

Indian Government even awarded Prof. Kramrisch with the Padma Bhushan for her contribution to the study, teaching and popularizing of Hindu art in the United States.[23] Sadly, no such accolade or recognition has come Louise's way from either the Indian or the Australian government, posthumously.[24]

Before her death, Louise donated boxes filled with her writings, books, dance compositions, audio material, notes on music and press clippings of her tours with Indian artists to the Music Archives at Monash University (Figure 6.3). In 1996, using some of the material from the Music Archives, renowned Indian-Australian dancer and choreographer Tara Rajkumar OAM created a dance and "dialogic performance" entitled *Temple Dreaming*.[25] This dance drama revived the memory of Louise Lightfoot and her passion for Kathakali.

Temple Dreaming was first performed in Australia at the Alexander Theatre at Monash University and later toured India. Tara observed that in this dance project she "moved from a strictly theatrical tradition of solo performance into an ensemble work and creating symbols totally new to the particular dance tradition."[26] This was a unique project created with the help of several Australian dancers and juxtaposed both the traditional and contemporary Western and Indian dancing styles. In an interview with Sunil Kothari, Tara observes:

Figure 6.3 Louise Lightfoot photographed displaying a hand gesture from Indian dance, 1978.

Source: Photograph from the Louise Lightfoot Bequest, Monash University.

Photograph Courtesy: Music Archives of Monash University and Mary Louise Lightfoot.

Until I opened the trunk stored in the archives of Monash University's Music department all those years ago, Louise Lightfoot had been nothing more than a name to me. But once I began delving through its contents—the diaries, papers and artistic mementoes—the spell was cast. I was so inspired by what I discovered from Lightfoot's mementoes that I created a dance theatre show about the life of this fascinating Australian expatriate.[27]

The Louise Lightfoot Collection of the Monash University Music Archives inspired her to create this performance project.

Each object that I looked at, each box that I opened, brought back memories of my training in Kerala, the southernmost state of India, and the powerful images of life and performance which had gripped me as a student learning Kathakali. Equally engrossing and personally involving were Lightfoot's biographical notes. There were so many points of contact that I identified with—people, places and references which belonged to my childhood's storehouse of memories.[28]

For Tara, creating a dance performance on Louise's life in India and her contribution to Hindu temple dance became a challenge. She writes:

How do I put across these closely shared references to an Australian audience of today which has very little association with any of these significant performance factors? How do I realise some of the excitement that Kathakali and the Temple Dances aroused in Lightfoot and captured her imagination? As I delved into her writings and records of her journeys, my journey into creating a performance started to assume a definite course.[29]

As she delved deeper into Louise's notes and drafted her own ideas about the performance project, Tara realized a few similarities between Louise and herself. She writes:

Being primarily a performer, I realised that Louise Lightfoot and I were fascinated by the same performance idiom and vocabulary. She was not a dancer and her ego was not that of a performer. In fact, she revelled in communicating this Eastern dance tradition, which she had discovered, to a totally alien and uninitiated Western audience. She wanted to take to the rest of the world the beauty and perfection she perceived in Kathakali when she arrived in Kerala. For me, this intense dedication and intrinsic love of a dance form, a performance idiom, a theatre tradition, became the common factor between the subject of my research and myself. I was born to it; she revived and pursued it with a passion.[30]

It became crucial for Tara to capture and re-create the Kathakali dance form for the audiences as faithfully as possible to the one originally seen by Louise in the villages of Kerala in the 1930s. The logic behind this was to use the dance theatre tradition and take the audience through a journey of discovery.[31] To achieve this, Tara created specific imagery and selected objects from the archives that can transport the audiences to Louise's first impressions of India. She writes:

> For example, a large metal box (trunk) found in the Louise Lightfoot Music Archives became an essential part of the performance. In it was a big chunk of the special life of Lightfoot which was turning into performance. The trunk, therefore, became symbolic of discovery. Contrary to traditional performances, *Temple Dreaming* began in the theatre foyer with a sculptural installation being signified with activated sound and light effects. The trunk became the base for the installation from which rose a figure capturing a fragment of the essence of the Dance of Siva, the dance that attracted Louise Lightfoot to India.[32]

The scenes were further helped by an activated voice that projected Louise's words from her journal explaining her immense love for India and Hindu temple dance.

As audiences move further into *Temple Dreaming* they are face to face with Tara. Her own story and the discovery of the Louise Lightfoot Collection is also part of the performance. She notes that the last scene of the performance reflects the arrival of dancers like herself into Australia. This not only highlights the changing nature of dance audiences and the art forms but also establishes a dance dialogue that suggests continuity.[33]

Thanks to Louise Lightfoot's pioneering spirit and dedication to Indian dance, the Indian subcontinent's classical dance in different styles is now regularly staged in various Australian cities by a number of re-sident multicultural dance companies along with ballet and con-temporary dance. Dance in Australia has in fact been shaped by her influence and ground-breaking work.

Today, Indian dance in Australia is celebrated and represented by professional dance artists, companies, schools and amateur community groups. These have, over the years, performed traditional Indian classical dances, Bhangra and Bollywood in various cultural festivals organized throughout Australia. Lightfoot's collaboration with Shivaram, Priyagopal and Ibetombi exposed Australian audiences to Indian dance. Their dance tours had "great cultural significance" and these dance performances, lectures and demonstrations "considerably enhanced the respect for the intellectual heritage of India."[34] Noticing the unfailing excitement among Australian audiences, the Arts Council also extended financial support to similar dance recitals subsequently.

In the end, however, Priyagopal and Ibetombi have been forgotten. But Shivaram's impact through Kathakali is acknowledged even today—something that even Louise did not expect to accomplish.[35] Shivaram, who moved in the social life of Australia, and charmed journalists and audiences alike, brought the two cultures closer and stimulated a period of vitality and originality through the Indian dance form.[36]

Notes

1 Khoni, "Dance Aesthetics of the Meeteis of Manipur," 9.
2 Founded in 1950, ICCR's main objective is to actively participate, foster, promote, and strengthen cultural relations between India and other countries (https://www.iccr.gov.in/).
3 Bandopadhay, "Manipuri Dance," 142.
4 Mathew, "A tête-à-tête with Bimbavati Devi, Manipuri Dance Exponent," 2004.
5 Kothari, "In praise of Guru Bipin Singh," 2017.
6 Since 1957, Darshana Jhaveri has performed more than thirty foreign tours organized by either the ICCR or private organisations.
7 In 2008, Sruti Bandopadhay performed Manipuri dances at a function organised by the Bengali Association in Brisbane, Queensland.
8 Padma Shri is the fourth-highest civilian award after the Bharat Ratna, the Padma Vibhushan and the Padma Bhushan.
9 For a detailed discussion on Indian dancer and capital pulls of the global stage, see Srinivasan, *Sweating Saris*, 141–164.
10 Lightfoot, *Lightfoot Dancing*, Chapter 29.
11 Kothari, "New Directions in Indian Dance," 2008; Fischer-Lichte, *Dionysus Resurrected*, 2013.
12 Zarrilli, *Kathakali Dance Drama*, 31.
13 Rupachandra, "Manipuri Dances," 2012. R. K. Danisana, brother of late Priyagopal, also published a book entitled *Manipuri Dances: A Panorama of Indian Culture* (2012).
14 Not much is known about Laishram Lakshman Singh's life but R. K. Tamphasana Devi notes that his unpublished memoir is in the custody of Prof. L. Loken Singh of D. M. College of Arts in Imphal, Manipur. See Tamphasana Devi, "The Tagore Family and the Manipuri Dance (1920–1960)," 13921–13922.
15 Samom, "Thokchom Ibetombi Devi," 2008.

16 Danisana, "R. K. Priyagopalsana as Cultural Beacon," 2013; Samom, "Thokchom Ibetombi Devi," 2008; "Smt. Kshetrimayum Ibetombi Devi," 2016.
17 Vishnudevananda Saraswati was founder of the International Sivananda Yoga Vedanta Centres and Ashrams. He established the Sivananda Yoga Teachers' Training Course, one of the first yoga teacher-training program in the West.
18 Lightfoot, *Lightfoot Dancing*, Chapter 36.
19 Lightfoot, "Lightfoot, Louise," 2008.
20 At Monash University, Louise Lightfoot successfully organised shows and workshops for Shivaram (1974 and 1976) and Sonal Mansingh (1976).
21 "… from India," 10.
22 Lightfoot, *Lightfoot Dancing*, Chapter 36.
23 See Miller, *Exploring India's Sacred Art*, 1983.
24 "Australian *Kathakali* Artiste Dead," *The Indian Express*, 2 July 1979.
25 Tara Rajkumar OAM, an accomplished Indian Mohiniattam and Kathakali dancer was conferred with the Medal of Order of Australia in 2009 for her contribution to multiculturalism and Arts in Australia.
26 Rajkumar, "Fragile Gesture," 36.
27 Kothari, "Australian Diary: Part 2," 2009.
28 Rajkumar, "Fragile Gesture," 36.
29 Ibid.
30 Ibid., 36–37.
31 Ibid., 37.
32 Ibid.
33 Ibid.
34 Artlover Madras, "Ananda Shivaram," 3.
35 Shaw, "Currently Narrating 'Kathakali' in Montreal," 1959.
36 Sarwal, *The Dancing God*, 2020.

Bibliography

"… from India." *Monash Reporter: A Magazine for the University*, July 5, 1976, 10.

"64 Drums – 1 Player." *The News*, August 14, 1951.

"Afghan cameleers in Australia." *Australian Stories*, September 3, 2009. Accessed July 7, 2017. http://www.australia.gov.au/about-australia/australian-story/afghan-cameleers

Ahmad, Aziz. *Studies in Islamic Culture in the Indian Environment*. Oxford, UK: Clarendon Press, 1964.

Ahmed, Y. Rafeek. "India's Membership of the Commonwealth: Nehru's Role." *The Indian Journal of Political Science* 52, no. 1 (1991): 43–53.

Aihara, Byron. "A Lesson with the Maibi of Manipur: Ima Dhoni Amaibi." *Seven Sisters Music*, May 9, 2016. Accessed September 25, 2019. http://sevensistersmusic.com/?p=175.

Alexander, Fred. "Indian Dancers." Letters to the Editor. *The West Australian*, July 12, 1951, 9.

Allen, Margaret. "Identifying Sher Mohamad: 'A Good Citizen.'" In *Empire Calling: Administering Colonial Spaces in India and Australasia*, edited by Ralph Crane, C. Vijayasree, and Anna Johnston, 103–119. New Delhi: Oxford University Press, 2013.

Allen, Margaret. "Observing Australia as the 'Member of an Alien and Conquered Race'." In *Reading Down Under: Australian Literary Studies Reader*, edited by A. Sarwal and R. Sarwal, 560–570. New Delhi: SSS Publications, 2009a.

Allen, Margaret. "Otim Singh in White Australia." In *Something Rich and Strange: Sea Changes, Beaches and the Littoral in the Antipodes*, edited by Susan Hosking, Rick Hosking, Rebecca Pannell, and Nena Bierbaum, 195–212. Adelaide: Wakefield Press, 2009b.

Allen, Matthew Harp. "Rewriting the Script for South Indian Dance." *The Drama Review* 41 (1997): 63–100.

Anand, Mulk Raj. "In Praise of Manipur." Editorial. *Marg* 14, no. 4 (September 1961): 2–3.

Anandhi, S. "Representing Devadasis: 'Dasigal Mosavalai' as a Radical Text." *Economic and Political Weekly* 26, nos. 11–12 (1991): 739–746.

Anderson, W. K., and S. D. Damle. *The Brotherhood of Saffron: The Rashtriya Swayamasevak Sangh and Hindu Revivalism*. New Delhi: Vistaar Publications, 1987.

Anoop, Maratt Mythili, and Varun Gulati, eds. *Scripting Dance in Contemporary India.* Maryland: Lexington Books, 2016.

Arambam, Lokendro. "Manipur: A Ritual Theatre State (Coronation Model and Concept of Welfare)." In *Manipur – Past and Present (Volume II)*, edited by Naorem Sanajaoba, 57–75. New Delhi: Mittal Publications, 1991.

Arambam, Lokendro. "Preface." In *Lammitlon: The Manipuri Toponomy (A Treatise of Place Names in Meitei)*, edited by M. Gourachandra. Kakching: The People's Museum, 2004.

"Artistry of Indian Dancers Thrills Devonport Audience." *The Advocate*, April 2, 1957.

Artlover Madras. "Ananda Shivaram: India's Cultural Ambassador – White Australia Applauds *Rukmangada.*" *The Indian Express*, June 6, 1949, 3.

Au, Susan, and Jim Rutter. *Ballet and Modern Dance.* London: Thames & Hudson, 2012.

Aurobindo, Sri. *The Secret of the Veda.* Vol. 10. Pondicherry: Sri Aurobindo Ashram, 1971.

"Australian Kathakali Artiste Dead." *The Indian Express*, July 2, 1979. News clipping. Accessed October 15, 2013. Louise Lightfoot Collection, Music Archives of Monash University.

B.B. "Indian Dancers Artistic." *Daily Telegraph*, June 7, 1957.

Bakhle, Janaki. "Country First? Vinayak Damodar Savarkar (1883–1966) and the Writing of Essentials of Hindutva." *Public Culture* 22, no. 1 (2010): 149–186.

Bandopadhay, Sruti. "Dance: The Tool of Sanskritisation Process in Manipur." *Ausdance*, July 18, 2008. Accessed May 4, 2014. http://ausdance.org.au/articles/details/dance-the-tool-of-sanskritisation-process-in-manipur

Bandopadhay, Sruti. "Manipuri Dance: A Lyrical Manifestation of Devotion." In *Dance Matters: Performing India on Local and Global Stages*, edited by Pallabi Chakravorty and Nilanjana Gupta, 140–149. New Delhi: Routledge, 2012.

Bandopadhay, Sruti. *Manipuri Dance: An Assessment on History and Presentation.* Gurugram: Shubhi Publication, 2010.

Banerjee, Sumanta. "'Hindutva': Ideology and Social Psychology." *Economic and Political Weekly* 26, no. 3 (1991): 97–101.

Banerjee, Utpal K. *Tagore's Mystique of Dance.* New Delhi: Niyogi Books, 2014.

Bapat, Guru Rao. *Re-scribing Tradition: Modernisation of South Indian Dance Dramas.* Shimla: IIAS, 2012.

Baruah, Sanjib. "India: The Mongolian Fringe." *Himal Southasian* 26, no. 1 (2013): 82–86.

Basu, Anustup. *Hindutva as Political Monotheism.* Durham, NC: Duke University Press, 2020.

Basu, Tapan, Pradip Datta, Sambuddha Sen, Sumit Sarkar, and Tanika Sarkar. *Khaki Shorts, Saffron Flags: A Critique of the Hindu Right.* Delhi: Orient Longman, 1993.

Bateson, Gregory. "Play and Paradigm." In *Play and Anthropological Perspectives*, edited by Michael A. Salter, 7–16. West Point: Leisure, 1977.

Bayly, Christopher. "India and Australia: Distant Connections." Keynote Address at the Australian Historical Association conference, Adelaide, July 9, 2012. Accessed May 4, 2014. http://www.theaha.org.au/wp-content/uploads/2015/08/Bayley-2012_India-and-Australia.pdf

Beaver, Moya. "Interview with Michelle Potter." National Library of Australia Oral History Collection, October 13, 1994. Accessed May 4, 2014. http://www.nla.gov.au/amad/nla.oh-vn513088/0-1891~0-2080

Bennett, Bruce, Santosh K. Sareen, Susan Cowan, and Asha Kanwar, eds. *Of Sadhus and Spinners: Australian Encounters with India*. New Delhi: HarperCollins, 2009.

Bilimoria, Purushottama. "Indian Dance." In *Currency Companion to Music and Dance in Australia*, edited by John Whiteoak and Aline Scott-Maxwell, 330–331. Sydney: Currency Press, 2003.

Bilimoria, Purushottama. "Of Dance & Theory: History of Indian Dance in Australia, from Lightfoot-Shivaram to Chandrabhanu." Paper Presented at Melbourne University South Asian Students Group, Melbourne, October 6, 2013. Accessed January 29, 2014. https://www.academia.edu/4766690/Of_Dance_and_Theory_History_of_Indian_Dance_in_Australia_from_Lightfoot-Shivaram_to_Chandrabhanu.

Bilimoria, Purushottama. "The Spiritual Transformation of Indian Dance in Australia – From Lightfoot to Aboriginal Corroboree." Paper Presented at the Conference on the Study of Religions of India: "Confounding and Contesting Religious and Cultural Boundaries," Knoxville, September 11–14, 2008.

Bilimoria, Purushottama. "Traditions and Transition in South Asian Performing Arts in Multicultural Australia." In *Culture, Difference and the Arts*, edited by Sneja Gunew and Fazal Rizvi, 108–129. Sydney: Allen and Unwin, 1994.

Biswas, Debanjali. "Hasta in Manipuri." Wednesday Wisdom - Blog. *Akademi*. June 2, 2020. Accessed July 25, 2020. https://akademi.co.uk/hasta-in-manipuri

"BJP Manipur Pradesh Vision Document 2017." State Vison Document Committee, Bhartiya Janta Party, 2017. Accessed August 15, 2021. https://ceomanipur.nic.in/documents/manifesto/BJP%20Manifesto.pdf

Bose, Mandakranta. "The Evolution of Classical Indian Dance Literature: A History of Sanskritic Tradition." PhD diss., Oxford University, 1989.

Bowers, Faubion. "Dance and Opera in Manipur." *The Atlantic Monthly* (October): 158–160.

Brara, N. Vijaylakshmi. *Politics, Society and Cosmology in India's North East*. New Delhi: Oxford University Press, 1998.

Brissenden, Alan, and Keith Glennon. *Australia Dances: Creating Australian Dance, 1945-1965*. Kent Town, SA: Wakefield Press, 2010.

Brockington, J. *The Sacred Thread: Hinduism in its Continuity and Diversity*. Edinburgh: Edinburgh University Press, 1996.

Broinowski, Alison. *About Face: Asian Accounts of Australia*. Melbourne: Scribe, 2003.

Broinowski, Alison. *The Yellow Lady: Australian Impressions of Asia*. Melbourne: Oxford University Press, 1996.

"Brouhaha over Bipin Singh." *Sruti*, 68 (May 1990): 15.

Card, Amanda. "History in Motion." PhD diss., University of Sydney, 1999.

Cass, Joan. *The Dance: A Handbook for the Appreciation of the Choreographic Experience.* Jefferson, NC: McFarland, 2004.

Catherine, K. "Interview with Louise Lightfoot." Transcript. Women's Section. *ABC*, July, 1951.

Chaki-Sircar, Manjusri. *Feminism in a Traditional Society: Women of the Manipur Valley.* New Delhi: Shakti Books, 1984.

Chakravorty, Pallabi and Nilanjana Gupta, eds. *Dance Matters: Performing India on Local and Global Stages.* New Delhi: Routledge, 2012.

Chakravorty, Pallabi. "From Interculturalism to Historicism: Reflections on Classical Indian Dance." *Dance Research Journal* 32, no. 2 (2000–2001): 108–119.

Chakravorty, Pallabi. *Bells of Change: Kathak Dance, Women and Modernity in India.* Calcutta: Seagull Books, 2008.

Chandra, Suresh. *Encyclopaedia of Hindu Gods and Goddesses.* Delhi: Sarup & Sons, 1998.

Chatterjea, Ananya. "Contestations: Constructing a Historical Narrative for Odissi." In *Rethinking Dance History: A Reader*, edited by Alexandra Carter, 143–156. New York: Routledge, 2013.

Chatterjea, Ananya. "Dance Research in India: A Brief Report." *Dance Research Journal* 28, no. 1 (1996): 118–123.

Chatterjea, Ananya. "In Search of a Secular in Contemporary Indian Dance: A Continuing Journey." *Dance Research Journal* 36, no. 2 (2004): 102–116.

Chatterjee, Partha. *Nationalist Thought and the Colonial World.* London: Zed Books, 1986.

Chelliah, Shobhana L. "Linguistics Asserting Nationhood through Personal Name Choice: The Case of the *Meithei* of Northeast India." *Anthropological Linguistics* 47, no. 2 (2005): 169–216.

Cleaver, David K. "Indian Dancing." Letters to Editor. *The Sydney Morning Herald*, June 13, 1957.

Clifford, John. "Here's a Dance that's Different." *The Australasian Post*, August 30, 1951, 16.

Coomaraswamy, A. K. *History of Indian and Indonesian Art.* London: Edward Goldston, 1927.

Coomaraswamy, A. K. *The Dance of Shiva.* New York: The Noonday Press, 1975.

Coorlawala, Uttara Asha. "Ruth St. Denis and India's Dance Renaissance." *Dance Chronicle* 15, no. 2 (1992): 123–152.

Coorlawala, Uttara Asha. "The Classical Traditions of *Odissi* and *Manipuri – Odissi: Indian Classical Dance Art* by Sunil Kothari; *Dances of Manipur: The Classical Tradition* by Saryu Doshi." Review. *Dance Chronicle* 16, no. 2 (1993): 269–276.

Craine, Debra, and Judith Mackrell. *The Oxford Dictionary of Dance.* Melbourne: Oxford University Press, 2010.

Cummins, Constance. "Indian Dancers Give Exotic Performance." *The Telegraph*, May 21, 1957.

"Dancer Collects Shells." *The Advocate*, April 4, 1957, 1.

"Dancer from India." *The West Australian*, July 11, 1951, 9.

"Dancers' Art Delights." *Examiner*, April 13, 1950, 5.

Dandré, Victor. *Anna Pavlova: In Art & Life*. New York: Arno Press, 1979.

Danisana, R. K. "R. K. Priyagopalsana as Cultural Beacon." In *The Other Manipur*, edited by Sharma, H. Dwijasekhar, 1113–1289. 6 Vols. New Delhi: Akansha Publishing House, 2013.

Danisana, R. K. *Manipuri Dances: A Panorama of Indian Culture*. New Delhi: Rajesh Publications, 2012.

Darwin, John. *Unfinished Empire: The Global Expansion of Britain*. London: Penguin, 2012.

Davis, Alexander E. "'A Shared History?' Postcolonial Identity and India-Australia Relations, 1947–1954." *Pacific Affairs* 88, no. 4 (2015): 849–869.

Davis, Richard S. "Introduction." In *Religions of India in Practice*, edited by David S. Lopez, Jr., 3–52. Princeton, NJ: Princeton University Press, 1995.

De Boehme, C. B. "Indian Dancers Show Great Artistry." *The News*, August 14, 1951.

De Lepervanche, Marie M. "The (Silent) Voices of Indian Colies: Early Indian Workers in the Australian Colonies." In *Bridging Imaginations: South Asian Diaspora in Australia*, edited by Amit Sarwal, 58–84. New Delhi: Readworthy Publications, 2013.

De Lepervanche, Marie M. *Indians in a White Australia*. Sydney: Allen and Unwin, 1984.

De Triana, Rita Vega. *Antonio Triana and the Spanish Dance: A Personal Recollection*. London: Routledge, 2016.

Deshpande, Satish. "From Development to Globalization: Shifts in Ideological Paradigms of Nation and Economy in the Third World." In *Meanings of Globalization: Indian and French perspectives*, edited by R. Melkote, 98–114. New Delhi: Sterling Publishers, 2001.

Desmond, Jane. "Dancing out the Difference: Cultural Imperialism and Ruth St. Denis's *Radha* of 1906." In *Moving History, Dancing Cultures. A Dance History Reader*, edited by Ann Dils and Ann Cooper Albright, 256–270. Wesleyan: Wesleyan University Press, 2001.

Devi, Ibetombi. "Manipuri Dance Presented Abroad." *The Ngasi: A Manipuri National Daily*, April 8, 1957.

Devi, Ragini. *Dance Dialects of India*. Delhi: Motilal Banarsidass, 1990.

Doniger, Wendy, and Martha C. Nussbaum, eds. *Pluralism and Democracy in India: Debating the Hindu Right*. Delhi: Oxford University Press, 2015.

Doshi, Saryu. "Editorial." In *Dances of Manipur*, edited by Saryu Doshi. Special Issue of *Marg* 41, no. 2 (December 1989): vii–xii.

Doshi, Saryu. "Editorial." In *The Drum and the Cymbal: Classical Dances of Manipur*, edited by Saryu Doshi. Special issue of *Marg* 41, no. 2 (March 1988): iii–v.

Doshi, Saryu. *Dances of Manipur: The Classical Tradition*. Martinez, CA: Gaudiya Vedanta Publications, 1989.

"Dynamic Indian Dancer Here." *The Age*, August 20, 1951.

E.D.H. "Two Indian Dancers Enthral Audience." *Courier-Mail*, May 18, 1957.

Earnshaw, John. "Lang, John (1816–1864)." *Australian Dictionary of Biography*. Canberra: National Centre of Biography, Australian National University, 1974.

Accessed July 7, 2017. http://adb.anu.edu.au/biography/lang-john-3985/text6301

Erdman, Joan. "Dance Discourses: Rethinking the History of the 'Oriental Dance'." In *Moving Words: Re-writing Dance*, edited by Gay Morris, 288–305. New York: Routledge, 1996.

Erdman, Joan. "Performance as Translation: Uday Shankar in the West." *Drama Review* 31, no. 1 (1987): 64–88.

Feuerstein, G., S. Kak, and D. Frawley. *In Search of the Cradle of Civilisation*. Wheaton, Ill: Quest Books, 1995.

Fidelio. "Dancer and Drummer: Notable Artists from India." *The West Australian*, July 13, 1951.

Fidelio. "Indian Pair Show Vivid Dance Art." 1957. News clipping. Accessed October 15, 2013. Louise Lightfoot Collection, Music Archives of Monash University.

Flood, Gavin D. *An Introduction to Hinduism*. Cambridge, UK: Cambridge University Press, 1996.

Fowler, Jeaneane D. *Hinduism: Beliefs and Practices*. East Sussex, UK: Sussex Academic Press, 1997.

"Friendly Indian Likes Us." *Sun Women's Magazine*, April 9, 1947.

Gandhi, M. K. "Why I Am a Hindu." *Young India*, October 20, 1927. Accessed February 27, 2019. https://www.mkgandhi.org/truthisgod/22hindu.htm

George, Vensus A. *Paths to the Divine: Ancient and Indian*. Washington: CRVP, 2008.

Gergan, Mabel D. and Sara H. Smith. "Theorizing Racialization through India's 'Mongolian Fringe.'" *Ethnic and Racial Studies* (2021): 10.1080/01419870.2021.1925319.

Ghosh, Partha S. *BJP and the Evolution of Hindu Nationalism: From Periphery to Centre*. Delhi: Manohar, 2000.

Ghosh, Santidev. "Tagore and Manipuri Dances." In *Something Old, Something New: Rabindranath Tagore 150th Birth Anniversary Volume*, edited by Pratapaditya Pal. Special issue of *Marg* 62, no. 3 (March 2011): 69–70.

Gibson, Josie. "Dancer's Dream Lives on." *Monash Magazine* 3 (Autumn-Winter 1999). Accessed April 9, 2013. http://www.monash.edu.au/pubs/monmag/issue3-99/item-05.html

Gould, William. *Hindu Nationalism and the Language of Politics in Late Colonial India*. Cambridge: Cambridge University Press, 2004.

Grau, Andrée. "Dancing Bodies, Spaces/Places and the Senses: A Cross-cultural Investigation." *Journal of Dance & Somatic Practices* 3, no. 1–2 (2011): 5–24.

Grierson, George A. "Bhakti-Marga." In *Encyclopaedia of Religion and Ethics*, edited by James Hastings, 539–551. New York: T. and T. Clark, 1940.

Griffin, Marion Mahoney. *The Magic of America*. Chicago: Art Institute of Chicago, 2007.

Grimwood, Ethel St Clair. *My Three Years in Manipur and Escape from the Recent Mutiny*. London: Richard Bentley and Son, 1891.

"Guru Bipin Singh Association India and Abroad." *Narthaki.com*, September 24, 2014.

Hall, Fernau. "The Contribution of Indian Dance to British Culture." Paper Presented at the Academy of Indian Dance Seminar, Commonwealth Institute, London, June 29-30, 1982. Accessed April 16, 2013. http://www.vads.ac.uk/large.php?uid=47970

Hall, Stuart. *Representation – Cultural Representations and Signifying Practices*. London: Sage, 1997.

Hanna, Judith Lynne. *Dance, Sex, and Gender: Signs of Identity, Dominance, Defiance, and Desire*. Chicago: University of Chicago Press, 1988.

Hardy, Friedhelm, *Viraha Bhakti: The Early History of Krishna Devotion in South India*. Delhi: OUP, 1983.

Hassan, M. Sajjad. "Understanding the Breakdown in North East India: Explorations in State-society Relations." *Working Paper Series No. 07-83*. London: DESTIN, London School of Economics and Political Science, 2007. https://www.files.ethz.ch/isn/136987/WP83.pdf

Heath, Deana. *Purifying Empire: Obscenity and the Politics of Moral Regulation in Britain, India and Australia*. Cambridge, MA: Cambridge University Press, 2010.

"Hindu Dancer Astounds with Muscle Control." *Advocate*, April 2, 1950.

Horosko, Marian. *Martha Graham: The Evolution of Her Dance Theory and Training*. Florida: University Press of Florida, 2002.

Hosking, Rick, and Amit Sarwal, eds. *Wanderings in India: Australian Perceptions*. Clayton: Monash University Press, 2012.

Hutton. Geoffrey, "Exotic Indian Dancer." *The Age*, April, 1957.

"Ibetombi – Biographical Note." *Star Dancers of India*. Adult Education Board Programme Booklet (Albany Town Hall). February 11, 1957. Accessed October 15, 2013. Louise Lightfoot Collection, Music Archives of Monash University.

Inden, Ronald. *Imagining India*. Oxford: Blackwell, 1992.

"Indian Dancer: Entrancing Display by Shivaram." *The West Australian*, February 16, 1948, 10.

"Indian Dancers." *Bulletin*, April 3, 1957.

"Indian Dances Fascinated Albany Audiences." February 15, 1957. News clipping. Accessed October 15, 2013. Louise Lightfoot Collection, Music Archives of Monash University.

"Indian Prince to Dance Here." *Daily News*, July 4, 1951.

"Indian Style for Their Curry, too." 1957. News clipping. Accessed October 15, 2013. Louise Lightfoot Collection, Music Archives of Monash University.

"Indian Temple Dancer." *The Sun*, March 2, 1957, 32.

Jackson, A. V. Williams. "The Persian Dominions in Northern India Down to the Time of Alexander's Invasion." In *Ancient India*, edited by E. J. Rapson, 319–334. Cambridge, UK: Cambridge University Press, 1922.

"Jagoi." *Bulletin*, February 20, 1952, 25.

Jain, Jyotindra. "India's Republic Day Parade, Restoring Identities, Constructing the Nation." In *India's Popular Culture: Iconic Spaces and Fluid Images*, edited by Jyotindra Jain, 60–75. Mumbai: Marg Publications, 2002.

Jean Shaw, "Currently Narrating 'Kathakali' in Montreal." *Montreal Star*, March 2, 1959.

Jhaveri, Angana. "The Raslila Performance Tradition of Manipur in Northeast India." Unpublished Disst. Michigan State University, 1986.

Jhaveri, Darshana and Kalavati Devi. *Manipuri Nartana*. Varanasi: Choukhamba Orientalia, 1978.

Jhaveri, Nayana. *Guru Bipin Singh*. Calcutta: Manipuri Nartanalaya, 1979.

Jones, William. "The Four Yugs and Ten Avatars of the Hindoos." In *The Missionary Register*, 266–271. London: L. B. Seeley, 1820.

Joshi, Sashi, and Bhagavan Josh. *Struggle for Hegemony in India 1920–47*. 3 vols. New Delhi: Sage Publications, 1994.

Jost, Diana Brenscheidt. *Shiva Onstage: Uday Shankar's Company of Hindu Dancers and Musicians in Europe and the United States, 1931–38*. Berlin: LIT Verlag, 2011.

Kabui, Gangmuei. *History of Manipur*. Delhi: National Publishing House, 1991.

Kamal. "Indian Dancing is a Highly Developed Art." *Farrago: Melbourne University Newspaper*, April, 1957. News clipping. Accessed. Louise Lightfoot Collection, Music Archives of Monash University, October 15, 2013.

Kathju, Manorama. "People and What They're Doing." *The Sunday Standard*, September 2, 1951.

Katrak, Ketu H. *Contemporary Indian Dance: New Creative Choreography in India and the Diaspora*. Hampshire: Palgrave Macmillan, 2011.

Kersenboom-Story, Saskia C. *Nityasumangali: Devadasi Tradition in South India*. Delhi: Motilal Banarsidass, 1987.

Khatun, Samia. *Australianama: The South Asian Odyssey in Australia*. New York: Oxford University Press, 2018.

Khelchandra, Ningthoujongjam. *History of Ancient Manipuri Literature*. Imphal: Manipuri Sahitya Parishad, 1969.

Khokar, Mohan. *Traditions of Indian Classical Dance*. Delhi: Clarion Books, 1979.

Khoni, Khangembam. "Dance Aesthetics of the Meeteis of Manipur: An Ethno-Philosophical and Ethno-Cultural Performance Study." PhD diss., Visva-Bharati, Santiniketan, 2015.

King, Anthony. "Spaces of Culture, Spaces of Knowledge." In *Culture, Globalization and the World System: Contemporary Conditions for the Representation of Identity*, edited by Anthony King, 1–39. Minneapolis: University of Minnesota Press, 1997.

King, Richard. "Orientalism and the Modern Myth of 'Hinduism'." *NUMEN* 46, no. 2 (1999): 146–185.

Klostermaier, Klaus K. *A Survey of Hinduism*. New York: SUNY Press, 2007.

Kothari, Sunil, ed. *Bharata Natyam*. Mumbai: Marg Publications, 2007.

Kothari, Sunil. "Australian Diary: Part 2 – Interview with Kathakali and Mohiniattam dancer Tara Rajkumar." *Narthaki*. August 17, 2009. Accessed March 4, 2019. http://www.narthaki.com/info/gtsk/gtsk9.html

Kothari, Sunil. "In praise of Guru Bipin Singh." Footloose and Fancy Free. *Narthaki.com*. August 30, 2017. Accessed July 25, 2020. https://narthaki.com/info/gtsk/gtsk152.html

Kothari, Sunil. "In praise of Guru Bipin Singh." *Narthaki*. Accessed October 2, 2019. August 30, 2017" http://www.narthaki.com/info/gtsk/gtsk152.html

Kothari, Sunil. "New Directions in Indian Dance: An Overview 1980-2006." *Ausdance*, July 18, 2008. Accessed September 3, 2017. http://ausdance.org.au/articles/details/new-directions-in-indian-dance

Kumar, Anu. "Meet Sujata and Asoka, the Indo-German dancers who charmed Hollywood in the 1950s." *Scroll*, August 21, 2016. Accessed April 4, 2019. https://scroll.in/reel/814533/meet-sujata-and-asoka-the-indo-german-dancers-who-charmed-hollywood-in-the-1950s

Lakhia, Kumudini. "Innovations in Kathak." In *New Directions in Indian Dance*, edited by Sunil Kothari, 60–69. Mumbai: Marg Publications, 2003.

Lightfoot, Louise. "A Few Stories of Shivaram by His Australian Impresario," Typed Notes. 1947. Accessed October 15, 2013. Louise Lightfoot Collection, Music Archive of Monash University.

Lightfoot, Louise. "Explanation of Items by Miss Lightfoot's Hindu Dance Group." 1947. Accessed October 15, 2013. Louise Lightfoot Collection, Music Archive of Monash University.

Lightfoot, Louise. "In Search of Manipur." *Triveni*, July, 1951. Accessed April 16, 2013. http://yabaluri.org/TRIVENI/CDWEB/insearchofmanipurjul51.htm

Lightfoot, Louise. "International Appeal of the Ballet." *The Hindu*, February 11, 1940.

Lightfoot, Louise. "Letter to Protector of Emigrants (Bombay)." June 20, 1951. Accessed October 15, 2013. Louise Lightfoot Collection, Music Archives of Monash University.

Lightfoot, Louise. "Letter to Rajkumar Priyagopal Singh." August 6, 1950. Accessed October 15, 2013. Louise Lightfoot Collection, Music Archives of Monash University.

Lightfoot, Louise. "Notes." *Ritual Music of Manipur*. Notes. New York: Folkways Records, 1960.

Lightfoot, Louise. "Two Thousand Years of Rhythm." *The Argus*, July 31, 1946: 16.

Lightfoot, Louise. *Dance-rituals of Manipur, India: An Introduction to Meitei Jagoi*. Hong Kong: The Standard Press, 1958.

Lightfoot, Mary Louise, and Marian Quartly. "Lightfoot, Louisa Mary (1902-1979)." *Australian Dictionary of Biography*. Melbourne: Melbourne University Press, 2005. Accessed June 17, 2012. http://adb.anu.edu.au/biography/lightfoot-louisa-mary-13046

Lightfoot, Mary Louise. "Lightfoot, Louise." *Dictionary of Sydney*. Sydney: State Library New South Wales, 2008. Accessed January 29, 2014. https://dictionaryofsydney.org/entry/lightfoot_louise

Lightfoot, Mary Louise. *Lightfoot Dancing: An Australian Indian Affair*. New York: Amazon Digital Services, 2015.

Lille, Dawn. *Equipoise: The Life and Work of Alfredo Corvino*. New York: Dance Movement Press, 2010.

Lipner, Julius. "On 'Hindutva' and 'Hindu-Catholic,' with a Moral for Our Times." *Hindu-Christian Studies Bulletin* 5, no. 1 (1992): 1–8.

Lipner, Julius. *Life and Thought of a Revolutionary*. New Delhi: Oxford University Press, 1999.

Lisam, Khomdon Singh. *Encyclopaedia of Manipur: Vols. 2–3* Delhi: Kalpaz Publications, 2011.

Lochtefeld, James G. *The Illustrated Encyclopedia of Hinduism: A-M.* New York: The Rosen Publishing Group, 2002.

Longkumer, Arkotong. "Playing the Waiting Game: The BJP, Hindutva, and the Margins of the Nation." In *Majoritarian State: How Hindu Nationalism is Changing India*, edited by Angana P. Chatterji, Thomas Blom Hansen and Christophe Jaffrelot, 281–296. New York: Oxford University Press, 2019.

Lorenzen, David N. "Who Invented Hinduism?" *Comparative Studies in Society and History* 41, no. 4 (1999): 630–659.

"Louise Lightfoot – Biographical Note." *Star Dancers of India.* Adult Education Board Programme Booklet (Albany Town Hall). February 11, 1957. Accessed October 15, 2013. Louise Lightfoot Collection, Music Archives of Monash University.

M.L. "Excitement in Art of Dancer." *The Sydney Morning Herald*, September 17, 1951, 5.

M.L. "Dancer Holds Secrets of Dying Art." Music and Theatre. *The Sunday Herald*, September 23, 1951, 1.

Maclean, Kama. "India in Australia: A Recent History of a Very Long Engagement." In *Wanderings in India: Australian Perceptions*, edited by Rick Hosking and Amit Sarwal, 20–35. Clayton: Monash University Press, 2012.

Maclean, Kama. *British India, White Australia: Overseas Indians, Intercolonial Relations and the Empire.* Sydney: UNSW Press, 2020.

Masselos, Jim. "Two Places and Three Times: Fragments Retrieved of India and Australia in the 1950s, 1960s and 1980s," *Postcolonial Studies* 18, no. 2 (2015): 133–144.

Massey, Reginald. *India's Dances: Their History, Technique, and Repertoire.* Delhi: Abhinav Publications, 2004.

Mathew, Febina. "A tête-à-tête with Bimbavati Devi, Manipuri Dance Exponent," *Narthaki.* October 13, 2004. Accessed September 25, 2019. http://www.narthaki.com/info/intervw/intrvw72.html

McCulloch, W. *Account of the Valley of Munnipore and of the Hill Tribes with a Comparative Vocabulary of the Munnipore and Other Languages.* Calcutta: Bengal Printing Company Ltd., 1859.

McDuie-Ra, Duncan. *Debating Race in Contemporary India.* New York: Springer, 2016.

Medcalf, Rory. "John Lang, Our Forgotten Indian Envoy." *The Spectator Australia*, March 31, 2010. Accessed July 7, 2017. https://web.archive.org/web/20100515040332/http://www.spectator.co.uk/australia/5880088/john-lang-our-forgotten-indian-envoy.thtml

Meduri, Avanthi. "Bharatha Natyam: What Are You?" *Asian Theatre Journal* 5, no. 1 (1988): 1–22.

Meduri, Avanthi. "Labels, Histories, Politics: Indian/South Asian Dance on the Global Stage." *Dance Research* 26, no. 2 (2008a): 223–243.

Meduri, Avanthi. "The Transfiguration of Indian/Asian Dance in the United Kingdom: Contemporary 'Bharatanatyam' in Global Contexts." *Asian Theatre Journal* 25, no. 2 (2008b): 298–328.

"Melbourne: Intercolonial Exhibition of Australasia 1866–67." Intercolonial and International Exhibitions, State Library of Victoria, June 30, 2017. Accessed 7 July 2017. http://guides.slv.vic.gov.au/interexhib/1866to67.

Mill, James. *The History of British India*. 3 vols. London: Baldwin, Cradock and Joy, 1817.

Miller, Barbara Stoller. *Exploring India's Sacred Art: Selected Writings of Stella Kramrisch*. Philadelphia: University of Pennsylvania Press, 1983.

Minerva. "Theatre Royal Begins New Page in Its History Tonight." Music and Drama. *The Mercury*, March 31, 1950: 22.

Mishra, Vijay. *Devotional Poetics and the Indian Sublime*. New York: SUNY Press, 1998.

Monier-Williams, Monier. *Hinduism*. London: SPCK, 1894.

Munsi, Urmimala Sarkar. "Boundaries and Beyond: Problems of Nomenclature in Indian Dance History." In *Dance Transcending Borders*, edited by Urmimala Sarkar Munsi, 78–98. New Delhi: Tulika Books, 2008.

Nag, Kalidas, and Debajyoti Burman, eds. *The English Works of Raja Rammohun Roy*. Calcutta, India: Sadharan Brahmo Samaj, 1947.

Nandy, Ashis. "The Demonic and the Seductive in Religious Nationalism: Vinayak Damodar Savarkar and the Rites of Exorcism in Secularizing South Asia." In *Heidelberg Papers in South Asian and Comparative Politics: Working Paper No. 44*, edited by Subrata K. Mitra, 1–10. Heidelberg: University of Heidelberg, 2009. Accessed February 15, 2019. https://core.ac.uk/download/pdf/32580976.pdf

Narayan, Shovana. *The Sterling Book of Indian Classical Dances*. New Delhi: New Dawn Press, 2004.

"National Seminar on 'Hinduism in Manipur' on 29-30 June 2018." *Manipur Times*, June 2, 2018. Accessed February 25, 2019, http://manipurtimes.com/national-seminar-on-hinduism-in-manipur-on-29-30-june-2018/

Nauriya, Anil. "The Savarkarist Syntax." *The Hindu*, September 18, 2014. Accessed February 15, 2019. https://www.thehindu.com/2004/09/18/stories/2004091803791000.htm

Nilabir, Sairem. "The Revivalist Movement of Sanamahism." In *Manipur – Past and Present (Volume II)*, edited by Naorem Sanajaoba, 109–126. New Delhi: Mittal Publications, 1991.

Niyogi-Nakra, Mamata. "Indian Dance outside India: The State of Art." In *Dance of India: History, Perspectives and Prospects*, edited by David Waterhouse, 309–315. Mumbai: Popular Prakashan, 1998.

NLA Dance. "Indian Dance in Australia." List. Canberra: National Library of Australia, January 1, 2010. Accessed January 29, 2014. http://trove.nla.gov.au/list?id=1230

O'Shea, Janet. "At Home in the World? The Bharatanatyam Dancer as Transnational Interpreter." *The Drama Review* 47, no. 1 (2003): 176–186.

O'Shea, Janet. *At Home in the World: Bharat Natyam on the Global Stage*. Middletown, CT: Wesleyan University Press, 2007.

Page, David. *Prelude to Partition: The Indian Muslims and the Imperial System of Control, 1920-1932*. Delhi: Oxford University Press, 1982.

Pandeya, Gayanacharya Avinash C. *The Art of Kathakali*. Allahabad: Kitabistan, 1961.

Paranjape, Makarand, and Sukalyan Sengupta, eds. *The Cyclonic Swami: Vivekananda in the West*. New Delhi: Samvad India, 2005.

Paranjape, Makarand, ed. *Swami Vivekananda: A Contemporary Reader*. New Delhi: Routledge, 2015.

Paranjape, Makarand. *Decolonization and Development: Hind Svaraj Revisioned*. New Delhi: Sage Publications, 1993.

Parpola, Asko. *The Roots of Hinduism. The Early Aryans and the Indus Civilization*. New Delhi: Oxford University Press, 2015.

Parratt, John. *Wounded Land: Politics and Identify in Modern Manipur*. Delhi: Mittal Publications, 2005.

Parratt, Saroj Nalini. *The Religion of Manipur: Beliefs, Rituals and Historical Development*. Calcutta: Firma KLM Private Ltd, 1980.

Pask, Edward H. *Ballet in Australia: The Second Act, 1940-80*. Melbourne: Oxford University Press, 1982.

Pask, Edward H. *Enter the Colonies Dancing: A History of Dance in Australia, 1835-1940*. Melbourne: Oxford University Press, 1979.

Pathak, Avijit. "BJP has Insulted My Hinduism." *The Wire*, April 7, 2019. Accessed April 10, 2019. https://thewire.in/religion/bjp-has-insulted-my-hinduism

Pattabhiraman, N. "The Trinity of Bharatanatyam: Bala, Rukmini Devi and Kamala." *Sruti* 48 (1988): 23–24.

Pearce, Pat. "Hindu Dance." Stage and Screen. *The Herald*, December 7, 1953.

Phanjoubam, Pradip. "Manipur: Fractured Land." *Where the Sun Rises when Shadows Fall: The North-east India*. Special issue of *International Centre Quarterly* 32, no. 2–3 (2005): 275–287.

Potter, Michelle. "Ballet." In *Currency Companion to Music and Dance in Australia*, edited by John Whiteoak and Aline Scott-Maxwell, 70–77. Sydney: Currency Press, 2003.

Prabhavananda, Swami, and Frederick Manchester. *The Spiritual Heritage of India*. Madras: Sri Ramakrishna Mission, 1981.

Prashad, Vijay. *The Karma of Brown Folk*. Minneapolis: University of Minnesota Press, 2000.

Pratt, Mary Louise. "Arts of the Contact Zone." *Profession* 91 (1991): 33–40. Accessed May 15, 2014. http://www.nieuweleescultuur.ugent.be/files/meer_lezen2_pratt.pdf

Prentiss, Karen Pechilis. *The Embodiment of Bhakti*. Cary: Oxford University Press, 2000.

Purie, R. D. "Dance Forms." Book Review. *India Today*, September 15, 1979. Accessed September 4, 2017. http://indiatoday.intoday.in/story/book-review-traditions-of-indian-classical-dance-by-mohan-khokar/1/427832.html

Purkayastha, Prarthana. "Dancing Otherness: Nationalism, Transnationalism, and the Work of Uday Shankar." *Dance Research Journal* 44, no. 1 (2012): 69–92.

Qureshi, Regula. "Whose Music? Sources and Contexts in Indic Musicology." In *Comparative Musicology and the Anthropology of Music*, edited by Bruno Nettl and Philip Bohlman, 152–168. Chicago: University of Chicago, 1991.

R.R. "Recital of Hindu Dances." *The Sydney Morning Herald*, June 13, 1957.

R.R. "Traditional Dances of India." *The Sydney Morning Herald*, June 7, 1957.

Rahman, Sukanya. *Dancing in the Family*. New Delhi: HarperCollins, 2002.

Rajkowski, Pamela. *In the Tracks of the Camelmen: Outback Australia's Most Exotic Pioneers*. North Ryde, NSW: Angus and Robertson, 1987.

Rajkumar, Tara. "Fragile Gesture: Indian and Western Approaches to Theatricality." In *World Dance '96: New Dance from Old Cultures*, 35–38. Melbourne: The Green Mill Dance Project, 1996.

Ramachandran, D. P. *Empire's First Soldiers*. Delhi: Lancer Publishers, 2008.

Ramnarayan, Gowri. "Rukmini Devi: Dancer and Reformer, a Profile." Part 2. *Sruti* 9 (1984b): 17–29.

Ramnarayan, Gowri. "Rukmini Devi: Restoration and Creation." *Sruti: Indian Classical Music and Dance Magazine* 10 (August 1984): 26–38.

Ram-Prasad, C. "Contemporary Political Hinduism." In *The Blackwell Companion to Hinduism*, edited by Gavin Flood, 526–550. Oxford, UK: Blackwell Publishing, 2003.

Ray, Sohini. "Boundaries Blurred? Folklore, Mythology, History and the Quest for an Alternative Genealogy in North-east India." *Journal of the Royal Asiatic Society* 25, no. 2 (April 2015): 247–267.

Ray, Sohini. "Writing the Body: Cosmology, Orthography, and Fragments of Modernity in Northeastern India." *Anthropological Quarterly* 82, no.1 (2009): 129–154.

Robinson, Harlow. *The Last Impresario: The Life, Times, and Legacy of Sol Hurok*. New York: Viking, 1994.

Rojio, Usham. "Subdued Eloquence: Poetics of Body Movement, Time and Space." In *Modern Practices in North East India: History, Culture, Representation*, edited by Lipokmar Dzüvichü and Manjeet Baruah, 275–308. New Delhi: Routledge, 2017.

Roy, Jyotirmoy. *History of Manipur*. Calcutta: Firma K. L. Mukhiopadhyay, 1958.

Russell, Elizabeth. "Louise Lightfoot: Dancing from East to West." *Dance Australia Magazine* 8 (1982): np.

Rutledge, Martha. "Inglis, James (1845-1908)." *Australian Dictionary of Biography*. Canberra: National Centre of Biography, Australian National University, 1972. Accessed July7, 2017. http://adb.anu.edu.au/biography/inglis-james-3834/text6087.

Sachau, Edward C., ed. and trans. *Alberuni's India*. 2 vols. London: Kegan Paul, Trench, Triibner & Co., 1914.

Sahai, Baldeo. *The Sterling Book of Essence of Indian Thought*. Delhi: Sterling Publishers, 2010.

Samom, Thingnam Anjulika. "Thokchom Ibetombi Devi: Traditional Music and Dance Exponent." *The Sangai Express*, January 3, 2008. Accessed October 15, 2013. http://www.e-pao.net/epSubPageExtractor.asp?src=features.Profile_of_Manipuri_Personalities.Thingnam_Anjulika.Thokchom_Ibetombi_Devi.

Sana, Rajkumar Somorjit. *The Chronology of Meetei Monarchs (From 1666 to 1850 CE)*. Imphal, India: Waikhom Ananda Meetei, 2010.

Sanajaoba, Naorem. *Manipur Past and Present*. Delhi: Mittal Publication, 2005.

Sanjeev, Thingnam. "Surveying and Producing the Frontier in Nineteenth Century Manipur: Challenges and Practices." *Asian Ethnicity* (2019). DOI: 10.1080/14 631369.2019.1585750

Sarkar, Sumit. *Beyond Nationalist Frames: Postmodernism, Hindu Fundamentalism, History*. Bloomington: Indiana University Press, 2002.

Sarwal, Amit, ed. and comp. *Louise Lightfoot in Search of India: An Australian Dancer's Experience*. Newcastle upon Tyne, UK: Cambridge Scholars Publishing, 2017.

Sarwal, Amit. "'A Kangaroo and Bradman': Indian Journalists' visit to Australia under the Colombo Plan, 1950-1957." *Journalism Studies* (2018). 10.1080/1461 670X.2018.1428907

Sarwal, Amit. *The Dancing God: Staging Hindu Dance in Australia*. London: Routledge, 2019.

Savarkar, Vinayak Damodar. *Hindutva: Who is a Hindu?* Bombay: Veer Savarkar Prakashan, 1969.

Scott-Maxwell, Aline. "Asia and Pacific Links." In *Currency Companion to Music and Dance in Australia*, edited by John Whiteoak and Aline Scott-Maxwell, 52–56. Sydney: Currency Press, 2003.

Sebastian, Rodney. "'Reverse Pilgrimage': Performance, Manipuri Identity, and the Ranganiketan Cultural Arts Troupe." In *Religious Journeys in India: Pilgrims, Tourists, and Travelers*, edited by Andrea Marion Pinkney and John Whalen-Bridge, 253–280. New York: SUNY Press, 2018.

Sebastian, Rodney. "Cultural Fusion in a Religious Dance Drama: Building the Sacred Body in the Manipuri Raslilas." PhD dissertation, University of Florida, 2019.

Sen, Geeti. "Return of the Prodigy." Interview. *India Today*, December 15, 1976. Accessed July 7, 2017. http://indiatoday.intoday.in/story/i-was-very-much-impressed-and-inspired-by-kathakali-ragini-devi/1/436881.html

Seymour, Alan. "Presenting Louise Lightfoot." *Western Mail*, February 12, 1948: 51.

Shah, Purnima. "State Patronage in India: Appropriation of the 'Regional' and 'National'." *Dance Chronicle* 25, no. 1 (2002): 125–141.

Shah, Raichand. "Letter to Rajkumar Priyagopal Singh." Accessed October 15, 2013. Louise Lightfoot Collection, Music Archives of Monash University.

Shakespear, J. "The Religion of Manipur." *Folklore* 24, no. 4 (1913): 409–455.

Sharma, Arvind. "On Hindu, Hindustān, Hinduism and Hindutva." *Numen* 49, no. 1 (2002): 1–36.

Sharma, Jyotirmaya. *Hindutva: Exploring the Idea of Hindu Nationalism*. New Delhi: HarperCollins Publishers India, 2015.

Sharma, Tejmani. "The Goddess of Dancing - Letter to Louise Lightfoot." May 3, 1957. Accessed October 15, 2013. Louise Lightfoot Collection, Music Archives of Monash University.

Singh, Bipin. "Abhinaya." *Marg* 14, no. 4 (September 1961): 15–29.

Singh, E. Nilakanta. "Contemporary Gurus and Artists." *Marg* 14, no. 4 (September 1961): 61–64.

Singh, E. Nilakanta. "Lai Haraoba." *Marg* 14, no. 4 (September 1961): 30–34.

Singh, E. Nilakanta. "Manipuri: Cause for Concern." *Indian Literature* 24, no. 6 (1981): 94–99.

Singh, Haobam Kulabidhu. *Manipuri Dances.* Sagolband, Manipur: Self-published, 1954a.

Singh, Haobam Kulabidhu. *Manipuri Raasas.* Sagolband, Manipur: Self-published, 1954b.

Singh, Haobam Kulabidhu. *The Art of Manipuri Dances.* Sagolband, Manipur: Chudachand Printing Works, 1955.

Singh, Kunj Bihari. "Manipur Vaishnavism: A Sociological Interpretation." *Sociological Bulletin* 12, no. 2 (September 1963): 66–72.

Singh, Mutua Jhulan. *Bejoy Punchalee: History of Manipur, Parts 1 and 2.* Calcutta: Saksena Printing Works, 1936.

Singh, N. Lokendra. *The Unquiet Valley: Society, Economy, and Politics of Manipur, 1891-1950.* New Delhi: Mittal Publications, 1998.

Singh, R. K. Achoubisana. "Lai-haraoba: The Gods Rejoice." In *Dances of Manipur,* edited by Saryu Doshi. Special Issue of *Marg* 41, no. 2 (December 1989): 11–18.

Singh, Rajkumar Priyagopal. "Letter to Louise Lightfoot." August 31, 1950. Accessed October 15, 2013. Louise Lightfoot Collection, Music Archives of Monash University.

Singh, Rajkumar Priyagopal. "Letter to Louise Lightfoot." July 2, 1945. Accessed October 15, 2013. Louise Lightfoot Collection, Music Archives of Monash University.

Singh, Rajkumar Priyagopal. "Letter to Louise Lightfoot." June 29, 1946. Accessed October 15, 2013. Louise Lightfoot Collection, Music Archives of Monash University.

Singh, Sanasam Gourahari. "Extract from 1970 Annual Function Report." *Parampara.* Ministry of Culture, Government of India. Accessed September 30, 2019. https://www.paramparaproject.org/institution_jawahar-manipuri-dance.html

Sinha, Smriti Kumar. "Rabindranath Tagore and the Bishnupriya Manipuri Community." Blog, 2011. Accessed September 25, 2019. https://smritikumarsinha.wordpress.com/rabindranath-tagore-and-the-bishnupriya-manipuri-community/

Sitlhou, Hoineilhing. "The Shifting 'Stages' of Performance: A Study of 'Chavang Kut' Festival in Manipur." *Asian Ethnicity,* 19, no. 4 (2018): 468–488.

Smith, Wilfred Cantwell. *Meaning and End of Religion.* New York: Macmillan, 1963.

"Smt. Kshetrimayum Ibetombi Devi." Grant for Art, 2016. Accessed September 15, 2017. http://grantforart.com/event/smt-kshetrimayum-ibetombi-devi/

Soneji, Davesh. *Unfinished Gestures: Devadasis, Memory, and Modernity in South India.* Chicago: University of Chicago Press, 2012.

Sorell, Walter. *Dance in its Time.* New York: Columbia University Press, 1986.

Srinivas, M. N. *Social Change in Modern India.* Delhi: Orient Longman, 1989.

Srinivasan, Amrit. "Reform and Revival: The Devadasi and her Dance." *Economic and Political Weekly* 20, no. 44 (1985): 1869–1876.

Srinivasan, Amrit. "Temple 'Prostitution' and Community Reform: An Examination of the Ethno graphic, Historical and Textual Context of the Devadasi of Tamil Nadu, South India." PhD diss., Cambridge University, 1984.

Srinivasan, Priya. *Sweating Saris: Indian Dance as Transnational Labor*. Philadelphia: Temple University Press, 2011.

Stevens, Christel. "Bringing Manipuri Dance to the World Stage." *E-Pao*, 2006. Accessed October 15, 2013. http://e-pao.net/epPageExtractor.asp?src=features. Manipuri_Dance_World_Stage.html

Sugirtharajah, Sharada. *Imagining Hinduism: A Postcolonial Perspective*. London: Routledge, 2003.

Sutch, W. B. "Ancient Dance Form." Letter to the Editor, 1951. Press clipping. Accessed October 15, 2013. Louise Lightfoot Collection, Music Archives of Monash University.

T. B. "Dancer & Drummer Portray India's Age-old Arts," 1951. Press clipping. Accessed October 15, 2013. Louise Lightfoot Collection, Music Archives of Monash University.

Tamphasana Devi, R.K. "Aspects on Louise Lightfoot's Attempt to Popularise Manipuri Dance in Australia, New Zealand and Japan (1938-1958)." *IOSR Journal of Humanities and Social Science* 22, no. 8.IV (August 2017): 45–48.

Tamphasana Devi, R.K. "The Tagore Family and the Manipuri Dance (1920-1960)." *International Journal of Development Research* 7, no. 07 (2017): 13919–13922.

"Temple Dancer Says Fiji an Indian's Paradise." *The Mail*, 4.

Ternan, Beatrice. "Dance Dramas." Letters to the Editor. *The Advertiser*, August 15, 1951, 4.

Terpsichore. "Indian Dancer." Letters to the Editor. *The West Australian*, July 11, 1951, 11.

Terry, Walter. *Ted Shawn: The Father of Modern Dance*. New York: Dial Press, 1976.

Thapar, Romila. "Some Appropriations of the Theory of Aryan Race relating to the Beginnings of Indian History." In *Invoking the Past: The Uses of History in South Asia*, edited by Daud Ali, 15–35. New Delhi: Oxford University Press, 1999.

Thapar, Romila. "The Theory of Aryan Race and India: History and Politics." *Social Scientist* 24, no. 1-3 (1996): 3–29.

Thapar, Romila. *Interpreting Early India*. Delhi: Oxford University Press, 1993.

Tharoor, Shashi. *Why I Am a Hindu*. Delhi: Aleph Book Company, 2018.

"The First Australian Ballet (1929-1950)." Trove, National Library of Australia, January 1, 2010. Accessed January 27, 2014. http://trove.nla.gov.au/people/ 671050

"The Language of Muscles." 1957. News clipping. Accessed October 15, 2013. Louise Lightfoot Collection, Music Archives of Monash University.

"The Passing Show." *The West Australian*, July 5, 1951, 7.

Thnag, Kungo. "Rabindranath Tagore and His Influence in Bishnupriya Manipuri Society." *Me and My Manipuri Things*, April 21, 2008. Accessed May 4, 2014. http://manipuri.wordpress.com/2008/04/21/rabindranath-tagore-and-his-influence-in-bishnupriya-manipuri-society/

Thobani, Sitara. *Indian Classical Dance and the Making of Postcolonial National Identities: Dancing on Empire's Stage.* New York: Routledge, 2017.

Turnbull, J., and P. Y. Navaretti, eds. *The Griffins in Australia and India: The Complete Works and Projects of Walter Burley Griffin and Marion Mahony Griffin.* Melbourne: Miegunyah Press, 1998.

"Two Dancers from Manipur." Dance and the Drama. *The ABC Weekly*, October 13, 1951, 15.

"Varied Crowd Looks at Temple Dancer." *The Advertiser*, August 14, 1951.

Vatsyayan, Kapila. "Introduction." In *Dances of Manipur*, edited by Saryu Doshi. Special Issue of *Marg* 41, no. 2 (December 1989): xii–xx.

Venkatraman, Leela. *Indian Classical Dance: The Renaissance and Beyond.* New Delhi: Niyogi Books, 2015.

Walker, David, and Agnieszka Sobocinska, eds. *Australia's Asia: From Yellow Peril to Asian Century.* Crawley: UWA Press, 2012.

Walker, David. "National Narratives: Australia in Asia." *Media History* 8, no. 1 (2002): 63–75.

Walker, David. *Anxious Nation.* St Lucia, Qld: University of Queensland Press, 1999.

Walker, David. *Experiencing Turbulence: Asia in the Australian Imaginary.* New Delhi: Readworthy, 2013.

Walker, David. *Stranded Nation: White Australia in an Asian Region.* Crawley, WA: UWA Publishing, 2019.

Watson, Anne, ed. *Beyond Architecture: Marion Mahony and Walter Burley Griffin – America, Australia, India.* Haymarket, NSW: Powerhouse Publishing, 1998.

Westrip, Joyce P., and Peggy Holroyde. *Colonial Cousins: A Surprising History of Connections between India and Australia.* Adelaide: Wakefield Press, 2010.

Whaling, Frank. *Understanding Hinduism.* London: Dunedin Academic Press, 2009.

Wilson, H. H. *The Religious Sects of the Hindus.* London: Christian Literature Society for India, 1904.

Yarrow, Ralph. *Indian Theatre: Theatre of Origin, Theatre of Freedom.* Surrey: Curzon, 2001.

Zubrzycki, John. *Jadoowallahs, Jugglers and Jinns: A Magical History of India.* New Delhi: Pan Macmillan India, 2018.

Zubrzycki, John. *The Last Nizam: An Indian Prince in the Australian Outback.* Melbourne: Pan Macmillan, 2006.

Index

Note: *Italic* page numbers refer to figures; page numbers followed by 'n' refer to notes.

www.ingramcontent.com/pod-product-compliance
Ingram Content Group UK Ltd.
Pitfield, Milton Keynes, MK11 3LW, UK
UKHW020416010325
455677UK00029B/903